The Power of Faith

by
John MacArthur, Jr.

WORD OF GRACE COMMUNICATIONS
P.O. Box 4000
Panorama City, CA 91412

Library of Congress Cataloging in Publication Data

MacArthur, John.
　　The power of faith / by John MacArthur, Jr.
　　　　p.　cm.　— (John MacArthur's Bible studies)
　　Selected from messages delivered at Grace Community Church in Panorama City, Calif.
　　Includes indexes.
　　ISBN 0-8024-5353-8
　　1. Faith—Biblical teaching.　2. Bible.　N.T.　Hebrews XI. I-XII.
4—Criticism, interpretation, etc.　I. Title.　II. Series:
MacArthur, John.　Bible studies.
BS2545.F3M33　1987
234'.2—dc19　　　　　　　　　　　　　　　　　　　　　　87-23163
　　　　　　　　　　　　　　　　　　　　　　　　　　　　　CIP

1 2 3 4 5 6 7 Printing/LC/Year 91 90 89 88 87

Printed in the United States of America

Contents

These Bible studies are taken from messages delivered by Pastor-Teacher John MacArthur, Jr., at Grace Community Church in Panorama City, California. These messages have been combined into a 10-tape album entitled *The Power of Faith*. You may purchase this series either in an attractive vinyl cassette album or as individual cassettes. To purchase these tapes, request the album *The Power of Faith*, or ask for the tapes by their individual GC numbers. Please consult the current price list; then, send your order, and make your checks payable to:

WORD OF GRACE COMMUNICATIONS
P.O. Box 4000
Panorama City, CA 91412

Or call the following toll-free number:
1-800-55-GRACE

1
What Is Faith?

Outline

Lesson
I. The Nature of Faith (v. 1)
  A. "The Substance of Things Hoped For"
    1. Faith's hope
      a) The hope of the Old Testament saints
      b) The hope of the Christian
        (1) Defies the system
          (*a*) Illustrated by Moses
          (*b*) Illustrated by Daniel's friends
        (2) Defies the senses
        (3) Defies present pleasure
    2. Faith's substance
      a) Romans 8:24-25
      b) Hebrews 11:13
  B. "The Evidence of Things Not Seen"
    1. Faith's action
    2. Faith's appropriation
      a) Spiritual faith
      b) Natural faith
II. The Testimony of Faith (v. 2)
  A. The Approval of God
  B. The Absurdity of Man
    1. The level of reason
    2. The leap of faith
      a) Philosophy
      b) Art
      c) Music
      d) Culture
      e) Theology
    3. The loss of options

III. The Illustration of Faith (v. 3)
    A. The Perception of Our Origin
    B. The Proposals About Our Origin
       1. By philosophers
       2. By scientists

Lesson

I. THE NATURE OF FAITH (v. 1)

"Now faith is the substance of things hoped for, the evidence of things not seen."

That verse is not, in the purest sense, a definition of faith. However, it does tell us some of the characteristics of faith. It tells us what faith is like rather than providing us with an explicit theological definition. The word *faith* is the Greek word *pistis*, which means "belief, trust, confidence."

A. "The Substance of Things Hoped For"

You may say, "But things hoped for don't have any substance—they're just hoped for!" What we believe in is what we hope for, yet faith gives these things a present substance.

1. Faith's hope

    a) The hope of the Old Testament saints

    Hebrews 11 shows us that in Old Testament there were many men and women who rested on nothing but the promises of God. God in effect said, "There's coming a Messiah, One who will finally take away sin. There's coming a day when Israel will have its own kingdom, when the Messiah will reign, and when the land will be restored." God said through Ezekiel, "Then will I sprinkle clean water upon you, and ye shall be clean. . . . A new heart also will I give you, and a new spirit will I put within you; and I will take away the stony heart out of your flesh, and I will give you an heart of flesh" (36:25-26).

God told the Old Testament saints He would gather them into the land and give them peace and safety. They never saw any of those promises come to fulfillment, but they still hoped for their fulfillment. Every Jewish mother longed to be the mother of the Messiah. The Jews hoped for the restoration of Jerusalem after it was destroyed. Today they're still hoping for greater freedom and liberty in Israel. They're still living in hope. That is what faith is—it is living in a hope that is so real that it's given substance in the present tense. The promises given to the Old Testament saints were so real that, even though they never saw them, they based their lives on them. The Old Testament promises related to the future, but the people acted as if they were in the present. They took God at His word and lived on the basis of that. These were people of faith—faith that gave present substance to what was in the future.

b) The hope of the Christian

Faith is not wistful longing, hoping that something will come to pass tomorrow. Faith is absolute, utter certainty. It defies everything that is normal.

(1) Defies the system

If we follow the world's standards and seek after the things that are readily visible to us we can receive some measure of comfort and prosperity. If we follow the standards of God, whom we've never seen or heard, we may experience pain, loss, discomfort, unpopularity, persecution—even death—but that which we hope for is given substance in the present by the intensity of our faith. It is faith that tells us it is better to suffer with God now—knowing what shall be—than to prosper with the world. Our faith, then, is faith against the world's system.

(a) Illustrated by Moses

Hebrews 11:26 says of Moses, "Esteeming the reproach of Christ greater riches than the trea-

9

sures in Egypt." Moses believed in the messianic hope, forsaking the treasures of Egypt to be persecuted for a Messiah that wouldn't come for several thousand years. He had such a positive hope in the future that it gave him an absolute substance in the present.

(b) Illustrated by Daniel's friends

In Daniel 3:13-18 Shadrach, Meshach, and Abed-nego are confronted with the choice of obeying King Nebuchadnezzar—who was alive, powerful, and tangible—or obeying an invisible God. If they didn't obey the king they would be thrown into a fiery furnace. An empiricist would have said, "It's no contest. I only accept what I see, so I'll bow down to the king." But the child of God says, "I'll obey God—even though I can't see Him—and face the fiery furnace."

(2) Defies the senses

Our faith rejects our senses for the sake of our hope. Many people say, "Take whatever you can get that meets the need of your senses." But the Bible says, "Don't believe your senses. Believe God, who can only be reached by faith."

(3) Defies present pleasure

A Christian sacrifices the pleasures of the present for the promises of the future. Epicurus, who was responsible for a group known as the Epicureans, said that the chief end of life was pleasure. He was not a hedonist as many people believe. He insisted that people take the long view—to find out what was most pleasant ultimately, not momentarily. He believed that that which may bring the most pleasure momentarily may bring the most pain ultimately. In a sense Epicurus was correct. As Christians, we live for ultimate pleasure. We choose to suffer in this world because we know we'll be glorified forever in the next.

10

Faith—Making a Present Substance Out of a Future Reality

Everyone enjoys things by faith. Have you ever enjoyed a vacation in January—even though you didn't leave until August? You may have pictured yourself floating on a raft in a pool, soaking up the sun. Or you may have pictured yourself on a river, reeling in a twelve-foot trout. Have you done that? When I was young, Christmas was more fun by faith than it was in actuality! We all have those experiences. I took a trip to Israel by faith long before I ever left. I walked those hills as I studied the Bible—even though I had never been there. By faith we enjoy in the present what is a future reality. That is exactly what the writer of Hebrews is saying. Faith is making a present substance out of a future reality.

2. Faith's substance

The word *substance* in verse 1 is the Greek word *hupostasis*. This word appears only two other times in the book of Hebrews. In 1:3 it's used to speak of Christ as the very essence of the Father. The other time it's used, in 3:14, it speaks of an assurance, a guarantee, or a title deed. That is exactly what substance is—essence and assurance. Faith, then, provides the firm ground on which we stand, waiting for the assurance of the fulfillment of the essence of God's promise. Faith believes God and depends on Him. It's the assurance that that which is promised has essence, content, and reality.

a) Romans 8:24-25—"For we are saved by hope. But hope that is seen is not hope; for what a man seeth, why doth he yet hope for? But if we hope for that which we see not, then do we with patience wait for it." If you believe that the future God has promised is sure, then you'll patiently wait. You won't get upset, rattled, and worried—you'll just wait. That's faith in a future reality with a present substance.

b) Hebrews 11:13—Referring to the time of Abraham and Sarah, Hebrews 11:13 says, "These all died in faith, not having received the promises but having seen them afar off, and were persuaded of them, and embraced them, and confessed that they were strangers and pilgrims on the earth." You may say,

11

"But they never saw heaven!" Yes, they did—with the eye of faith. They embraced it and said, "We don't belong here. We're just pilgrims going to a city 'whose builder and maker is God' " (v. 10). Faith gives present reality—something to hold on to in the present—to something that is in the future. Faith gives us a future object and a security—an assurance that holds us fast.

B. "The Evidence of Things Not Seen"

1. Faith's action

The word *evidence* in Greek is *elenchos*, which means "conviction." Faith is the conviction that the unseen exists. That's what the author is saying. This phrase goes a little further than the first phrase in verse 1, because this phrase implies action. This is banking your life on your hope. Faith is living on the basis of things not seen.

When Thomas saw Christ after His resurrection, Christ said to him, "Thomas, because thou hast seen me, thou hast believed; blessed are they that have not seen, and yet have believed" (John 20:29). That's true faith. Faith in the first phrase of verse 1 actualizes a future truth; in the second phrase it commits a life to it. It's the conviction of things not seen.

Noah and the Two Sides of Faith

Noah believed God. God said, "Noah, it's going to rain." That didn't mean anything to Noah because he had never seen rain! (For an explanation, see p. 61.) That would be like God saying to you, "It's going to gleep." You'd say, "Pardon me?" It wouldn't make sense because the word *gleep* doesn't have any meaning to you. But God said, "Noah, it's going to rain. Water is going to drop out of the sky." Noah believed God—even though he had never seen rain. That which God promised became a reality to him because he believed. That's the first step. It was the "substance of things hoped for" in his mind.

But Noah didn't stop there. He built a boat. That's the conviction that takes it a step further. It was one thing to dream about what

12

rain might be like, but it was something else to establish his life on it and build a ship in the desert for 120 years. Noah not only believed what God said but he banked his life on it. I'm sure that there were times during that 120 years that Noah asked himself, *What am I doing?* But he not only believed what God said, he acted on it. That is what we're going to see all through Hebrews 11—faith believes and then acts.

2. Faith's appropriation

   a) Spiritual faith

   Christians believe God to the point that they bank their lives on Him. To the unbelieving world, to bank one's life on an invisible, spiritual, future belief looks preposterous. A nonbeliever may say, "You are just believing in 'pie in the sky.' " But a Christian can respond, "This world is not my home; I'm just passing through. My treasures are laid up in heaven."

   Paul says in Ephesians 2:6, "And [Christ] hath raised us up together, and made us sit together in heavenly places in Christ Jesus." In Ephesians 1:3 he says, "Blessed be the God and Father of our Lord Jesus Christ, who hath blessed us with all spiritual blessings in the heavenlies." As Christians, we're moving around in another domain—by faith—and the world believes that something is wrong with us. We worship "him who is invisible" (Heb. 11:27), and we bank our lives on Him. That's faith with a spiritual content—it has no visible verification. The natural man can't comprehend that kind of spiritual faith. Why? Because he has no spiritual perception.

   b) Natural faith

   There is a sense in which all men live by a principle of natural faith.

   (1) Drinking water—We drink water out of our faucets without knowing anything about what's in it.

(2) Canned food—We eat canned food and believe that the label states the truth about its contents.

(3) Money—We use money by faith. Money isn't worth near what it's supposed to be worth. Survivors of the economic crash in 1929 know that it wasn't a loss of cash that brought the depression; it was a loss of faith in cash. People stopped believing in money.

(4) Scientific experiments—A scientist exercises natural faith, not only in believing that his chemicals are labeled correctly, but also in believing that they won't explode when he mixes them.

(5) Surgical procedures—If you went to your doctor and he said, "You've got a problem that requires surgery," you would probably say, "OK," without totally understanding what he's talking about. Once in surgery you would lie on a table unconscious, allowing a medical team to work on you. That takes faith.

(6) Road signs—When we drive, we believe and follow the road signs.

Everyone operates on a principle of natural faith, but not everyone experiences saving faith, because that takes spiritual faith, a supernatural gift from God. Ephesians 2:8 says, "For by grace are ye saved through faith; and that not of yourselves, it is the gift of God." Spiritual faith is a gift of God; natural faith comes at birth. Romans 10:17 says, "Faith cometh by hearing, and hearing by the word of God [lit., "hearing a speech about Jesus Christ"]." If a person hears with a willing heart, prepared by the Holy Spirit, God will grant him the faith to respond. It's a gift from God. First Corinthians 1:21 says, "For after that, in the wisdom of God, the world by wisdom knew not God, it pleased God by the foolishness of preaching to save them that believe." The preaching of the cross brings faith when it reaches fertile soil in the heart of a person. Faith in a natural sense is one thing, and faith in a spiritual sense is something else.

The writer of Hebrews tells us the nature of faith. Faith is the ability to actualize something in the future and then to be able to bank your life on it. The unbelieving person has that in a physical sense but not in a spiritual sense—only those who know Jesus Christ do.

II. THE TESTIMONY OF FAITH (v. 2)

"For by it [faith] the elders [the Old Testament saints] received witness."

A. The Approval of God

The phrase "received witness" is from the Greek verb meaning "to receive praise" or "to receive approval." The Old Testament saints named in chapter 11 were praised or approved by God because they lived by faith. God approves those who operate on faith; and I believe there's a sense in which every person who lives by spiritual faith in God has within his own heart the knowledge of the approval of God. Don't you sense a peace and an assurance of reality when you trust God? I believe all Christians sense His approval.

The writer of Hebrews lists the Old Testament heroes of faith in chapter 11 and shows that they trusted in what they couldn't see, banking their lives on it. Hebrews 11:6a says, "Without faith it is impossible to please him." No matter what you do, you can't please God without faith. But if you have faith, God is pleased—He approves.

B. The Absurdity of Man

The man who lives in this world without faith lives a hopeless existence that doesn't have any answers. Imagine not believing in anything. Imagine blinding yourself to the issue of what will happen after you die. Imagine living in a world that is so black that there is no hope—and believing that you're a nothing in a universe that has no meaning. If there's no God outside this world, then existence has no meaning, no point, no purpose, and we're trapped in a cruel joke.

Modern man has put himself in a dilemma. What happens to a man when he doesn't have faith in God?

1. The level of reason

For many years people had what was called a unified field of knowledge. In other words, people understood God, history, science, and so on, within one frame of reference—the frame of reality. But then rationalistic biblical critics began attacking everything supernatural. They first attacked the Bible, wiping out everything that had even a taint of the miraculous. Rationalism reduced man to one level of existence—the level of reason.

That was difficult for people to handle. In a world that was purely rational and logical, people were considered nothing more than machines. People began to say, "This is terrible. I can't believe that. My soul longs for something out there—I must believe in something. I can't believe I'm just a machine without any ultimate meaning."

2. The leap of faith

A man named Søren Kierkegaard split the field of knowledge into two levels: reason and faith. But the level of faith did not necessarily involve content. One could believe in anything. You could believe in believing. Philosophers called this "the leap of faith." Many couldn't live in a world of reason so they jumped into the world of faith and believed in anything. One of the secrets of this philosophy is that you never have to tell what you leaped onto—it's your own private leap. This is irrational, illogical, existential contentlessness. How can a person live in a tension like that? Well, that's what people have done today.

For many years people lived with a rationalistic world view—everything was in a box. Then people started to take their leaps of faith. And when they started jumping, everything went.

a) Philosophy—The first thing to go into the level of faith was a myriad of strange philosophies.

b) Art—At one time art was reasonable. Paintings were realistic. But all of a sudden painters began painting pictures that looked like nothing anybody had ever seen before. Modern art became man's leap.

c) Music—When music took a leap we ended up with music that didn't have any rhyme, reason, or sense to it.

d) Culture—Culture also leaped to maintain its existence, and authors began writing works that smashed morality, ethics, love, and honesty.

e) Theology—The last thing to take a leap was theology. One man said, "Guess what? God died." And everything took a leap into nothingness—the area of the absurd.

3. The loss of options

When people don't have anything to believe in they are led to the absurd. Do you know why people take drugs today? They've run out of rational options, so they try to find an escape from a world of reason that leads to nowhere. People are grabbing onto reincarnation, witchcraft, astrology, and all kinds of strange beliefs because they've lost rational options. People have eliminated God along with everything else. That is what happens to the person who cannot have a content-oriented, substantial faith in God.

You don't need to jump into the absurd; there is a God you can put your faith in. You don't need to believe in believing; you can believe in the God who made the universe. There have been people from the time of Adam who have believed in God, and life for them had meaning, substance, and the conviction of a future reality. Believing in God gives a reason for living. People who do not believe in God get trapped in the absurd and have no meaning in their lives.

.

III. THE ILLUSTRATION OF FAITH (v. 3)

"Through faith we understand that the worlds were framed by the word of God, so that things which are seen were not made of things which do appear."

A. The Perception of Our Origin

The writer of Hebrews was saying to the Jews, "When I tell you that you must have faith, I'm not asking you to muster up something you can't. You already have faith that God is, that He made the world and the universe. You have a beginning of faith."

Belief that the visible world, the universe, and the ages were created by God is a conviction of faith—not sight. No one knows the origin of the world by sight. No one can say, "I was there when it happened and saw how it all started." The only thing we know about creation is what we know by faith. So the writer of Hebrews simply said, "Through faith we understand [perceive with intelligence] that the worlds [all that exists] were framed by the word [a specific utterance] of God." Moses taught that in Genesis. The writer of Hebrews was simply establishing that faith was not foreign to his Jewish readers. Why? Because by faith they believed that God made the world.

B. The Proposals About Our Origin

1. By philosophers—The origin of the universe is a problem that philosophers can't solve. English philosopher Bertrand Russell wrote a book entitled *Why I Am Not a Christian* (New York: Simon and Schuster, 1957). In it he gave some weak arguments against Christianity. Here's a sample:

   "I say quite deliberately that the Christian religion . . . has been and still is the principal enemy of moral progress in the world. . . . The whole conception of God is derived from the ancient Oriental despotism . . . a conception quite unworthy of free men" (pp. 21, 23). He believed we must conquer the world by intelligence. Yet in his autobiography, written near the end of his life, Russell expressed disillusionment with philosophy. He had no answers.

2. By scientists—You may say, "Scientists know how the universe began. Philosophers might not know, but scientists know." Scientists do not know how the universe began. Scientists can only observe and tell what is going on—not why. Science simply discovers laws that already exist. But unfortunately science tries to do what it can't do—observe things before they existed. Science cannot do that. Science *can* say, "That is a rock," or, "That is a chemical." But it cannot say where that rock or chemical came from or why it came. It only knows what it observes. Science has no access to the "why" of anything. There's nothing wrong with good, observable science; but it cannot explain how the universe began. Philosophers and scientists can't discover what we as Christians can, because by faith we know that God made the worlds.

Nobody x Nothing = Everything?

Evolution is based on the absurd principle that nobody x nothing = everything. Even evolutionists are trying to figure out what they're saying. G. A. Kerkut, a respected evolutionist, wrote *Implications of Evolution* (New York: Pergamon, 1960). He criticizes scientific dogmatism on the subject, and after examining the various implications of the theory of evolution, he concludes that the evidence is lacking (pp. viii, 150f).

Kerkut observes, "Most students become acquainted with many of the current concepts in biology whilst still at school and at an age when most people are, on the whole, uncritical. Then when they come to study the subject in more detail, they have in their minds several half truths and misconceptions which tend to prevent them from coming to a fresh appraisal of the situation. In addition, with a uniform pattern of education most students tend to have the same sort of educational background and so in conversation and discussion they accept common fallacies and agree on matters based on these fallacies" (p. 156).

I read a quote from one evolutionary scientist who said that since he rejected the idea of a creator God, evolution was the only other alternative he had. Another scientist said that to talk of the evolution of thought from sea slime to amoeba, and from amoeba to a self-conscious thinking man, means nothing—it is the easy solution of the thoughtless mind. Genesis 1 says that God made everything. "Through faith we understand that the worlds were framed by the word of God." That's something that even some of the most educated people in our world haven't learned yet.

The whole concept of trying to explain everything without God is a fool's effort. We understand by faith. Faith comprehends that which the human mind, no matter how brilliant, cannot understand. First Corinthians 2:9 says, "But as it is written, Eye hath not seen, nor ear heard, neither have entered into the heart of man, the things which God hath prepared for them that love him." Paul is saying two things. "Eye hath not seen, nor ear heard" speaks to physical perception or empiricism. "Neither have entered into the heart of man" speaks to rationalism. Man does not know by science or by philosophy the truth of God. Verse 10 says, "But God hath revealed them unto us by his Spirit." Faith not only comprehends God and the creation of the universe but it also comprehends salvation in Jesus Christ.

Focusing on the Facts

1. What are some synonyms for the word *faith* (see p. 8)?
2. What were some of the promises God made to the Old Testament saints (see pp. 8-9)?
3. Describe the hope of the Christian (see pp. 9-10).
4. Why should Christians be willing to suffer in this world (see p. 10)?
5. What are two aspects of Noah's faith (see pp. 12-13)?
6. In what sense do all people live by faith (see pp. 13-14)?
7. How does saving faith differ from natural faith (see p. 14)?
8. What are some of the results of man's refusal to exercise faith in God (see pp. 16-17)?
9. Was the concept of faith foreign to those addressed in the book of Hebrews? Explain (Heb. 11:3; see p. 18).
10. Why must all views of the origin of the universe be based on faith (see p. 18)?

Pondering the Principles

1. Daniel's three friends and Moses illustrate an important aspect of faith: it counts the cost. Moses forsook all the comforts and honor that were his as the adopted son of Pharaoh's daughter on account of his faith. Daniel's friends risked a horrifying death in a fiery furnace on account of their faith. In our day thousands of Christians in other countries face persecution, imprisonment, or death on account of their faith in Christ. What about you? Are you ready to take a stand for your faith no matter what the cost? Spend some time examining your life. Do you find some areas (such as family, work, or friends) where you are not willing to pay the price for your faith? If so, ask God to give you the boldness to stand firm in your faith in all areas of your life.

2. As Christians, our faith has content. Our faith is not a "leap in the dark" but is based on specific facts. How well do you know the facts upon which your faith rests? Are you familiar with the evidence showing that Jesus was an actual historical person who rose from the dead? Could you explain to a non-Christian why you accept the reliability of the Bible? How would you answer someone who claimed evolution is a proven scientific fact that renders belief in God unnecessary? The answers to those and other questions are waiting for you in your local Christian bookstore or church library in the apologetic section. Make use of them!

3. The Old Testament saints are commended for their faith in God's promises. God's promises are a treasury of comfort and hope for all believers. In fact, Peter refers to them as "precious and magnificent promises" (2 Pet. 1:4, NASB*). You may have sung the hymn "Standing on the Promises," but before you can take a stand on them, you must first know what they are. Make a list this week of all the promises of God you find in your daily Bible reading. Then praise God for each one, and begin to count on them.

*New American Standard Bible.

2
Abel and the Life of Faith

Outline

Introduction

Review

Lesson
I. Abel Offered a More Excellent Sacrifice (v. 4a)
   A. The Revelation of God's Established Pattern
      1. There was an established place of worship
      2. There was an established time for worship
      3. There was an established way to worship
   B. The Response to God's Established Pattern
      1. The response of Abel—obedient faith
      2. The response of Cain—disobedient works
   C. The Recognition of God's Established Pattern
      1. The basis of the life of faith
      2. The beginnings of the life of faith
II. Abel Obtained Righteousness (v. 4b)
   A. The Evidence of Abel's Faith
      1. John 8:30-31
      2. James 2:14-24
      3. Ephesians 2:10
   B. The Evidence of God's Approval
      1. Delivered to Abel
      2. Denied to Cain
   C. The Evidence of Cain's Unrighteousness
      1. He became angry
      2. He abandoned God's grace
      3. He murdered Abel
      4. He avoided the Lord

     5. He failed to repent

     6. He became an apostate

III. Abel Openly Spoke, Though Dead (v. 4c)

  A. To God

  B. To Cain

  C. To All People

     1. One comes to God by faith, not works

     2. One cannot follow reason and ignore revelation

     3. Sin is severely punished in the one who doesn't obey

Introduction

Biblical scholar James Moffatt once wrote that death is never the last word in the life of a righteous man. When a man dies, whether righteous or unrighteous, he leaves something in the world. He may leave something that will grow and spread like a cancer, or he may leave something that permeates the atmosphere with blessing like the fragrance of perfume. Dead men *do* tell tales. They are not silent; they speak. It was said of Abel, "He being dead yet speaketh" (Heb. 11:4c).

If Abel is still speaking, what is he saying? What does this man who lived when the earth was new have to offer us? Certainly the economy of God in his day was different than it is now. What does he say to us? Hebrews 11 talks about faith. And that is the message that Abel gives us—the message of faith.

Review

In our last lesson we looked at verses 1-3 and saw four features of faith: (1) it gives a present reality to a future fact (pp. 8-12); (2) it furnishes enough conviction to bank our lives on it (pp. 12-15); (3) it secures the blessing and the approval of God (pp. 15-17); and (4) it enables us to understand why so many philosophers and scientists of the world cannot understand and perceive the things that are not open to the senses (pp. 18-20).

Were Adam and Eve People of Faith?

In the purest sense Adam and Eve were not people of faith. They did not hope in what they had not seen. They walked and talked with God in the cool of the day in the Garden of Eden, and they had the presence of the Shekinah glory. In other words, their experience with God was real. It was on earth, but nevertheless they personally saw the manifestation of God. Before the Fall, they personally communed with God, and they knew Him in the fullest sense. Therefore, there was little faith involved before the Fall. That is why the writer of Hebrews didn't choose to use Adam and Eve as illustrations of faith. Instead, his first illustration of faith is Abel. Abel was born outside of Eden, so he never had the opportunity to know God as personally as his parents had. Therefore, when he believed God, he became the first illustration of faith. Abel was the first man of faith.

Lesson

Hebrews 11:4 says, "By faith Abel offered unto God a more excellent sacrifice than Cain, by which he obtained witness that he was righteous, God testifying of his gifts; and by it he being dead yet speaketh." This text is divided into three progressive points. Abel's faith led him to do three things: (1) to offer a more excellent sacrifice; (2) to obtain righteousness; and (3) to openly speak, though dead. Because he believed he offered a better sacrifice. Because he offered a better sacrifice he obtained righteousness. Because he obtained righteousness he is, for all ages, a living voice saying, "Righteousness comes by faith."

I. ABEL OFFERED A MORE EXCELLENT SACRIFICE (v. 4a)

To understand this verse in Hebrews 11, we must go back to Genesis 4 and study the record of Cain and Abel. Verse 1 says, "Adam knew [sexual intimacy that produces a child] Eve his wife; and she conceived, and bore Cain, and said, I have gotten a man from the Lord." The name *Cain* probably comes from the Hebrew word *qana*, which means "to get." There is a play on words in verse 1. Using the meaning of the name *Cain* it reads, "Adam knew Eve his wife; and she conceived, and bore 'to get,' and said, I have gotten a man from the Lord." If you want to take the term "to get" and put it in a context that makes it obvious what she is saying, she actually names the baby "he is here." In other words, she says, "I have gotten 'he is here.' " She is probably trying to say that perhaps this is the Deliverer who will open the way back to God as promised in 3:15. But Eve was wrong. Cain turned out to be a murderer.

Verses 2-4 say, "She again bore his brother, Abel. And Abel was a keeper of sheep, but Cain was a tiller of the ground. And in process of time it came to pass, that Cain brought of the fruit of the ground an offering unto the Lord. And Abel, he also brought of the firstlings of his flock and of the fat thereof. And the Lord had respect unto Abel and to his offerings."

A. The Revelation of God's Established Pattern

Genesis 4:3-4 says that Cain and Abel each brought a sacrifice. That tells us several things.

1. There was an established place of worship

The fact that both Cain and Abel "brought" their offerings "unto the Lord" indicates that God had established some place where they were to bring their offerings. I believe that it's possible that this place was east of Eden, where God had placed an angel with a flaming sword to keep anyone from going back in the Garden (cf. 3:24). It seems that this was the established point of contact with God. Also, there's good indication that there was already an altar there since verse 4 says that Abel brought a sacrifice that was already slain. God, even though He expelled man from the Garden, here provided a mercy seat, like the later Mercy Seat in Israel that was covered by cherubim.

2. There was an established time for worship

Verse 3 says, "In process of time it came to pass." If you take that apart in the Hebrew it literally means "at the end of days." In other words, at the end of a certain prescribed time, it was time for a sacrifice. Perhaps God had revealed a special day for atonement. Since God is a God of order, it's likely that He had established a time when Cain and Abel were to come and worship Him. I believe this is also indicated by the fact that they both came at the same time and that they both seemingly had information regarding this sacrifice.

3. There was an established way to worship

God could be approached only by sacrifice. The children of Adam and Eve had been instructed that there was a place and a time for offering sacrifices. I believe that pre-supposes that they had also been instructed that there was a way to sacrifice. Cain and Abel wouldn't have known anything about the way to sacrifice if God hadn't told them, because the concept of sacrifice appears here for the first time. They came together at the same time in the same place—but they came with different offerings. The fact that God only accepted one of these offerings indicates that God had already established a pattern.

B. The Response to God's Established Pattern

1. The response of Abel—obedient faith

Hebrews 11:4 says that Abel offered his sacrifice by faith. Where does faith come from? Romans 10:17 says, "Faith cometh by hearing." A person can't put his faith in what he does not know. Therefore, to assume that Abel offered a sacrifice by faith also assumes that God told him what He wanted and that Abel believed and obeyed God. God told Abel He required a sacrifice—Abel believed and evidenced his faith by doing what God said to do.

What Was Wrong with Cain's Offering of Fruit?

There's nothing wrong with offering God fruits, vegetables, and grain. Leviticus 19:24 says, "But in the fourth year all the fruit thereof shall be holy with which to praise the Lord." God at times accepted fruit offerings. But the fruit was never offered before a blood sacrifice. A blood sacrifice always had to be made first because it was necessary to deal with sin before one could enter God's presence. There were bloodless meal offerings, but the blood sacrifice had to be made first to deal with sin. When Abel did

27

what God said, he revealed his obedience and acknowledged his sinfulness. Cain was disobedient and didn't acknowledge his sin.

Hebrews 11:4 says, "By faith Abel offered unto God a more excellent sacrifice than Cain." Abel's sacrifice was better because it was a blood sacrifice. It is important to realize that God had prescribed this; otherwise Abel would have had no idea what he was doing. If Abel just happened to offer the right offering by accident, then what right did he have to be called righteous? If Abel brought a sheep because he was a shepherd, and Cain brought tomatoes because he was a gardener, on what arbitrary basis would God say, "Abel, you're righteous. Cain, you're not"? That would be tantamount to God's saying, "I like sheep, but I can't stand tomatoes." The fact that Abel's sacrifice was accepted means that he heard what God said and obeyed. Otherwise there is no premise for his righteousness. Abel believed God and said, "God, this is what You said You wanted. You said if I brought this You'd forgive my sin. I brought it, and I believe You, God. I acknowledge my sin, and I acknowledge the prescribed remedy."

2. The response of Cain—disobedient works

Cain had the same information that Abel had, yet he brought what he wanted anyway. Cain didn't believe God. Instead, he thought he could approach God by his own works. He gathered up the fruit that he had grown, brought it to God, and said, "Here, God. Isn't it wonderful?" Cain's response to God's established pattern identifies him as the father of false religion. Why? Because false religion is an attempt to come to God by another way than that which God has prescribed. Peter says in Acts 4:12, "Neither is there salvation in any other; for there is no other name under heaven given among men, whereby we must be saved." False religion says, "Yes, there is. I can do whatever I want and just be good. If I have enough 'good points' I'll get there." Cain was the father of this. God said, "Do it this way," but Cain said, "No, I'll come my own way." That's false religion. False religion is an invented way to God. Proverbs 16:25 says, "There is a way that seemeth right unto a man, but the end thereof are the ways of death."

First, Cain failed to acknowledge the fact of sin. Second, he failed to obey God by bringing what God prescribed for his sin. He thought he could come on his own merit by the scheme he had invented. God rejected him, and he left the presence of the Lord and dwelt in the land of Nod (which means "wandering" or "roaming"), had children, and built the first city ever built. This was the birth of the world's system that fell under the control of Satan. Cain chose to go his own way and walked out of the presence of God (4:16). Don't feel sorry for Cain because God didn't accept his fruit. He knew what God wanted—he just wanted to do it his own way.

God's righteousness is not arbitrary; it is based on obedience to His prescribed plan. It was not a matter of ignorance with Cain; it was a matter of willful sin. Abel was righteous; Cain was not. This is supported by 1 John 3:11-12, which says, "For this is the message that ye heard from the beginning, that we should love one another. Not as Cain, who was of that wicked one, and killed his brother. And why killed he him? Because his own works were evil, and his brother's righteous." It wasn't arbitrary on God's part. To disobey is evil; to obey is righteous. It's that simple.

When Did God Initiate Sacrifices?

There is some indication that a sacrifice occurred, at least in part, in Genesis 3:21, where the Lord's action speaks about sacrifice: "For Adam also and for his wife did the Lord God make coats of skin, and clothed them."

Four things are intimated by the fact that God made cloaks of skin for Adam and Eve:

1. Sinners need to be covered.
2. The covering couldn't be humanly manufactured. Adam and Eve had already made a covering of leaves for themselves, but God said, "No, I will design the covering."
3. God had to provide the covering Himself.
4. The covering was obtained only by death. An animal had to die.

In a limited way, this was the initial disclosure of the importance of the sacrifice for covering.

C. The Recognition of God's Established Pattern

1. The basis of the life of faith

   Faith presupposes divine revelation. Someone who says "I believe in believing" is foolish. So also is someone who says, "It doesn't matter what you believe; just believe in anything. Believe whatever you want to believe." Faith presupposes a divine standard. Cain believed in himself—the wrong thing to believe in. Hebrews 9:22 says, "Without the shedding of blood there is no forgiveness" (NASB). I don't care what you believe; there is a standard, and God set it. Leviticus 17:11 says, "For it is the blood that maketh an atonement for the soul." That's a standard, a revelation, a disclosure from God. It's not arbitrary; it's absolute. People may say to me, "You're so narrow-minded." I could be broad-minded and tell lies, but that wouldn't help anyone. This is God's standard, and that's why I speak it.

2. The beginnings of the life of faith

   The life of faith begins with a sacrifice for sin. It begins when you admit you're a sinner, that you're worthy of death, and that you need His forgiveness, and you accept God's revealed plan. No man ever lives his life believing in God until he comes to God. And the only way a man ever comes to God is when he comes through the prescribed sacrifice of Christ, recognizing that he's a sinner. There's no other way. I'm not saying this to be narrow-minded; I'm saying it because it's the truth.

   In Genesis 4 the way to the cross is firmly established. Abel's lamb was the first lamb—one lamb for one man. Later on, in the Passover, it became one lamb for one family. Still later, on the Day of Atonement, it became one lamb for one nation. And finally, at Calvary, it became one Lamb for the world. Here in Genesis, with the first lamb, the way to the cross began to be paved.

Abel offered a better sacrifice. Why? Because it was out of obedience, it was of faith, it was given willingly, and he brought his best ("the firstlings of his flock"). Because Abel brought a more excellent sacrifice, several things resulted.

II. ABEL OBTAINED RIGHTEOUSNESS (v. 4b)

Genesis 4:4-5a says, "Abel, he also brought of the firstlings of his flock and of the fat thereof. And the Lord had respect unto Abel and to his offering; but unto Cain and to his offering he had not respect."

A. The Evidence of Abel's Faith

God didn't respect Abel merely for what was in Abel. God didn't say, "Abel, I like you better. I've checked you two over, and you're the best." There is nothing in the text to indicate that Abel was any better than Cain. They were both sinners. The only thing that obtained righteousness for Abel was that he did what God told him. Cain did not. That's the only difference. In fact, that's the only thing that changes man's relationship to God. It's not how good you are that matters; it's that you come to God on His terms. That's all He asks. Abel was as much a sinner as Cain, but he believed God and obeyed. Because of that, faith was counted to him for righteousness, and God accepted him. It's obedient faith that enables God to move in on our behalf and make us righteous. True faith is always obedient.

1. John 8:30-31—"As he spoke these words, many believed on him. Then said Jesus to those Jews who believed on him, If ye continue in my word, then are ye my disciples indeed." Many people have superficial faith, but the ones who obey are the ones who are true believers. Don't say you believe God and then disobey. If you believe God, obey.

2. James 2:14-24—In this passage James shows that true faith is always evidenced by works. For example, if a man says he believes but won't help a brother in need, his faith is dead. True faith always issues in works. Then James uses the illustration of Abraham and Isaac, showing that Abraham evidenced his true faith in his willingness to obey God to the point of sacrificing his

son. In verse 24 he sums up by saying, "Ye see, then, that by works a man is justified, and not by faith only." Does this contradict Paul? No. What it means is that visibly, in the eyes of people, your faith is only real when it issues in works. You can't work to get to God; but after having come to Him, works will become the evidence of true faith.

3. Ephesians 2:10—"We are his workmanship, created in Christ Jesus unto good works, which God hath before ordained that we should walk in them."

Abel evidenced the validity of his faith by obedience. I'm sure if someone asked Cain if he believed in God, he would have said, "Oh, yeah, I believe in God." But he didn't obey God, so God didn't respect his offering. First Samuel 2:30*b* says, "For them who honor me I will honor." There's no way to honor God apart from honoring Jesus Christ. That's His prescribed way.

B. The Evidence of God's Approval

1. Delivered to Abel

Hebrews 11:4 says that Abel received witness or approval from God. How did God do that? I believe God consumed his offering. The reason I believe that is there are at least five other occasions when God showed His approval by sending fire to consume the sacrifice: Leviticus 9:24, Judges 6:21, 1 Kings 18:38, 1 Chronicles 21:26, and 2 Chronicles 7:1. It's likely that this happened in Genesis 4, although it doesn't say specifically. But if that is how God showed approval of Abel's sacrifice, then fire fell on Abel's and didn't fall on Cain's.

When God approved of what Abel did, He imputed His righteousness to him. That's a miracle because Abel wasn't righteous. Neither are any of us. But when we believe in Jesus Christ, God imputes Christ's righteousness to us. Second Corinthians 5:21 says, "He hath made him, who knew no sin, to be sin for us, that we might be made the righteousness of God in him." This is the same thing that happened to Abel. He walked away from that altar a sinner with the same problems he had before he came. But God said, "Abel, you obeyed Me, so I impute My righteousness to you."

2. Denied to Cain

Cain did not have righteousness imputed to him. Self-styled works and a failure to acknowledge sin are never accepted by God (cf. Jude 11). According to C. I. Scofield in his comment on Jude 11 in the *New Scofield Reference Bible*, "Cain is an example of the religious natural man who believes in God, and in 'religion,' but after his own will, and who rejects redemption by blood." Romans 10:3-4 says, "For they, being ignorant of God's righteousness, and going about to establish their own righteousness, have not submitted themselves unto the righteousness of God. For Christ is the end of the law for righteousness to everyone that believeth." People try to establish their own righteousness when all they need to do is believe, and God will impute His righteousness.

C. The Evidence of Cain's Unrighteousness

1. He became angry

Genesis 4 tells us that when Cain didn't receive approval from God he became furious. Verse 5 says, "Cain was very angry, and his countenance fell." When a religious egotist gets put down, that is hard for him to handle.

2. He abandoned God's grace

"The Lord said unto Cain, Why art thou angry? And why is thy countenance fallen?" God moves toward Cain, revealing His redemptive character. Verse 7 says, "If you do well, will not your countenance be lifted up? And if you do not do well, sin is crouching at the door; and its desire is for you, but you must master it" (NASB). God was saying, "Look, Cain, this isn't the end. If you come back again and do it right—if you offer the right sacrifice in obedient faith—you will be accepted just as your brother. But if you don't, sin waits at your door like a crouching beast ready to spring up and destroy you. You must overcome that." In grace, God was extending to Cain an offer to come back. But Cain didn't want to—he wasn't interested. He knew what was required, yet he willingly rejected it.

3. He murdered Abel

Verse 8 says, "Cain talked with Abel his brother: and it came to pass, when they were in the field, that Cain rose up against Abel, his brother, and slew him." This was the first death in human history. From the apparent conversation, Abel was totally unsuspecting. Cain yielded to Satan, who, in John 8:44, is referred to as "a murderer from the beginning."

4. He avoided the Lord

Verse 9 says, "The Lord said unto Cain, Where is Abel, thy brother? And he said, I know not: am I my brother's keeper?" Cain not only lied to God and denied what he had done, but he also was sarcastic.

5. He failed to repent

In verses 10-12 Cain is accused, convicted, cursed, and sentenced for the murder of his brother. Verse 13 says, "Cain said unto the Lord, My punishment is greater than I can bear." In other words, "I can't stand this, God. You're overdoing it." There was no penitence, no sorrow for sin, no pleading for grace, no desire to give the right sacrifice. Cain pitied himself. It's interesting that sinners often pity themselves and blame God. In verse 14 Cain continues, "Behold, thou hast driven me out this day from the face of the earth; and from thy face shall I be hidden; and I shall be a fugitive and a wanderer in the earth; and it shall come to pass, that any one that findeth me shall slay me." Cain was sad, but he wasn't repentant. Remorse is one thing, and repentance is another. Remorse is being sorry you got caught; repentance is turning around and changing. Cain was sad, but he wasn't repentant.

6. He became an apostate

   Verse 16 says, "Cain went out from the presence of the Lord, and dwelt in the land of Nod, on the east of Eden." Cain was the first apostate. He turned his back on God and walked away. He forfeited the God of grace.

Because Abel brought a more excellent sacrifice he was able to obtain righteousness.

III. ABEL OPENLY SPOKE, THOUGH DEAD (v. 4c)

Hebrews 11:4 says, "He being dead yet speaketh." To whom did Abel speak?

A. To God—Genesis 4:10 says, "Thy voice of thy brother's blood crieth unto me from the ground." Cain thought he had stilled his brother's voice, but his brother's blood cried to God. What did it cry for? Vengeance (cf. Rev. 6:9-10).

B. To Cain—Genesis 4:11 says, "Now art thou cursed from the earth, which hath opened her mouth to receive thy brother's blood from thy hand." The soil itself bore the consciousness of his brother's blood. Every barren stretch of land, every weed, every handful of dirt all through Cain's life was the voice of his murdered brother crying out, indicting him.

C. To All People—Abel preaches a three-point sermon to all people.

   1. One comes to God by faith, not works.

   2. One cannot follow reason and ignore revelation. A person must abide by God's standard and obey it.

   3. Sin is severely punished in the one who doesn't obey.

Abel continues to preach a timeless sermon: "The just shall live by faith" (Heb. 10:38).

Focusing on the Facts

1. True or false: Adam and Eve were not truly people of faith (see p. 25).
2. What three things do we learn about Abel's faith (see p. 25)?
3. What does Genesis 4:3-4 tell us about worship in the time of Cain and Abel (see pp. 26-27)?
4. Why was Cain's offering not accepted by God (see pp. 27-28)?
5. In what sense was Cain the father of all false religion (see p. 28)?
6. True or false: Cain sinned out of ignorance of God's requirements (see p. 29).
7. Why is it significant that God made cloaks of animal skins for Adam and Eve (see pp. 29-30)?
8. What is the basis of our faith (see p. 30)?
9. True or false: God accepted Abel's sacrifice rather than Cain's because Abel was a better person (see p. 31).
10. What is one of the evidences of true faith (James 2:14-24; see pp. 31-32)?
11. What did God do for Abel after accepting his sacrifice (see pp. 32-33)?
12. What was Cain's reaction when his sacrifice failed to receive God's approval (see p. 33)?
13. True or false: God offered Cain another chance to bring an acceptable offering (see pp. 33-34).
14. True or false: Cain expressed repentance for his sin after God pronounced judgment on him (see p. 34).
15. What is Abel's message to us (see p. 35)?

Pondering the Principles

1. Cain's problems began when he offered God unacceptable worship. When you go to church, is the worship you offer to God acceptable? The following questions will help you determine that: Am I sincere? Is my attention focused on God? Am I coming to worship God, knowing His acceptance of me is based solely on what Christ has done for me? Am I coming with a pure heart, having dealt with any sin in my life? Am I coming to be a spectator or a participant?

2. Although Abel is dead, his life is still an example for us today. What kind of an example is your life setting for those around you? Does your faith affect each area of your life, or like Talkative in *The Pilgrim's Progress* are you a saint abroad and a devil at home? Do you work "heartily, as to the Lord" (Col. 3:23), or is the name of God blasphemed because of you (Rom. 2:24)? If there is an area of your life in which you are not setting a good example for others to follow, confess it to the Lord, and ask for His help to change.

3

Enoch and the Walk of Faith

Outline

Introduction
A. Abel's Worship of Faith
B. Enoch's Walk of Faith

Lesson
I. Enoch Believed in God
  A. The Basis of Pleasing God
    1. What doesn't please God
      a) Religion
      b) Nationality
      c) Good deeds
    2. What does please God
  B. The Beginning of Faith
    1. Enlightenment regarding God's existence
    2. Evidence regarding God's existence
      a) From science
        (1) The principle of cause and effect
        (2) The second law of thermodynamics
        (3) The evidence of design
      b) From reason
II. Enoch Sought God's Reward
  A. The Search
    1. 1 Chronicles 28:9*b*
    2. Psalm 58:11*a*
    3. Psalm 119:10*a*
    4. Proverbs 8:17
    5. Proverbs 11:18*b*
    6. Jeremiah 29:13
  B. The Specifics

Introduction

The Holy Spirit in Hebrews 11 begins with Abel and goes through the history of the Old Testament saints, showing that they came into a relationship with God by faith. God never intended works as a way to Himself; He intended works to issue from the salvation that took place when one approached Him on the basis of faith. As the Holy Spirit moves through the history of the people of the Old Testament who exhibited faith, He mentions first of all Abel, who illustrates worship by faith. Next He mentions Enoch, who illustrates the walk of faith.

Genesis 5:21-24 says, "Enoch lived sixty and five years, and begot Methuselah. And Enoch walked with God after he begot Methuselah three hundred years, and begot sons and daughters. And all of the days of Enoch were three hundred sixty and five years. And

Enoch walked with God, and he was not; for God took him." Remember that Adam and Eve had walked and talked with God in the cool of the day. But after they were thrown out of the Garden they ceased to walk with God. However, the destiny of man is re-instituted in the man Enoch, who stands as an illustration for all people of what it is to walk with God, experiencing the fellowship that Adam and Eve forfeited.

In Hebrews 11 there is a definite continuity. It begins with Abel's worship of faith—as he approached God by faith, bringing the proper sacrifice—and then continues with Enoch's walk of faith.

A. Abel's Worship of Faith

The life of faith begins on the basis of a proper sacrifice. A man cannot come to God and say, "God, I'm deciding to walk with You." The only way he'll ever walk with God is after he first comes to God on the basis of a sacrifice; and the only sacrifice that opens up the way to God is the sacrifice of Jesus Christ. Abel is the illustration of this principle. He came to God and worshiped through sacrifice. The next example in Hebrews 11 moves one step further in the process, and we find a man walking with God. First there's a death for sin; then there can be a walk with God. Enoch illustrates that.

B. Enoch's Walk of Faith

Enoch's faith included everything that constituted Abel's faith. I'm sure that Enoch offered a sacrifice to God, because a man can't come to God apart from the shedding of blood. Enoch did everything Abel did and took it even further—he walked with God. This principle hasn't changed. Men have to deal with their sin before they can walk with God.

"By faith Enoch was translated that he should not see death, and was not found, because God had translated him; for before his translation he had this testimony, that he pleased God. But without faith it is impossible to please him; for he that cometh to God must believe that he is, and that he is a rewarder of them that diligently seek him" (Heb. 11:5-6).

41

There are five features of Enoch's life of faith that pleased God: (1) Enoch believed in God; (2) he sought God's reward; (3) he walked with God; (4) he preached for God; and (5) he entered God's presence.

Lesson

I. ENOCH BELIEVED IN GOD

Hebrews 11:6 says, "But without faith it is impossible to please him; for he that cometh to God must believe that he is."

A. The Basis of Pleasing God

God was pleased with Enoch because he believed in Him. This is where the walk of faith begins—believing that God is. It is faith that pleases God.

1. What doesn't please God

   a) Religion—For the most part, God hates religion because it is a system developed by Satan to counteract the truth.

   b) Nationality—The Jews believed that because they were of the seed of Abraham, circumcised the eighth day, and possessors of the law of God, they were pleasing God. But that wasn't true; they displeased God greatly.

   c) Good deeds—Good deeds are not a way to God. Romans 3:20*a* says, "Therefore, by the deeds of the law there shall no flesh be justified in his sight." God isn't pleased with anyone who tries to earn his way into heaven. In fact, that kind of self-righteousness nauseates God.

2. What does please God

   Faith is what pleases God. Ephesians 2:8-9 says, "For by grace are ye saved through faith; and that not of yourselves, it is the gift of God—not of works, lest any man should boast." It is faith alone that pleases God, not religion, nationality, or works. Enoch pleased God because he lived by faith. In fact, he pleased God so much that one day he took a walk with God and they kept on walking—right into heaven!

B. The Beginning of Faith

Where does faith begin? It begins in the statement, "Believe that he is." That is not saying that a man just has to believe there is a God; it's saying he must believe that He is the only true God—not just any god or some god. Someone may say, "I believe in the 'Big Man upstairs,' " or, "I believe in the 'Happy Hunter in the happy hunting ground.' " No. You must believe that the God who claims to be God is all that He claims to be.

1. Enlightenment regarding God's existence

There's only one way a person can know God—by faith. No man can know God by sight. John 1:18a says, "No man hath seen God at any time." People sometimes say, "I had a vision. I saw God." No, they didn't. The Bible says no man has ever seen God. The closest anybody ever got to seeing God was in seeing Jesus Christ. In John 14:9b Jesus says, "He that hath seen me hath seen the Father." But that was in terms of essence. Since no man has ever seen God, nobody's going to come along and say, "I believe in God because I've seen Him." The only way God can be known is by faith, not sight.

In Job 38:2-6 God asks Job, "Who is this that darkeneth counsel by words without knowledge? Gird up now thy loins like a man; for I will demand of thee, and answer thou me. Where wast thou when I laid the foundations of the earth? Declare, if thou hast understanding. Who hath laid the measures of it, if thou knowest? Or who hath stretched the line upon it? Whereupon are its foundations fastened? Or who laid its cornerstone?" In other words, God was saying, "Job, you don't know anything except what you know by faith—you weren't around. You don't have any answers except the answers that I give you—and you either believe them or you don't."

2. Evidence regarding God's existence

a) From science

You can't prove God scientifically. It can't be done. At best, all scientific evidence is only circumstantial. Paul Little said, "It can be said with equal emphasis that you can't 'prove' Napoleon by the scientific method. The reason lies in the nature of history itself and in the limitations of the scientific method. In order for something to be 'proved' by the scientific method, it must be repeatable. One cannot announce a new finding to the world on the basis of a single experiment. . . . But history in its very nature is unrepeatable. No man can 'rerun' the beginning of the universe or bring Napoleon back or repeat the assassination of Lincoln or the crucifixion of Jesus Christ. But the fact that these events can't be 'proved' by repetition, does not disprove their reality as events" (*Know Why You Believe* [Downers Grove, Ill.: InterVarsity, 1968], p. 8). You can't apply the scientific method to everything; it doesn't work. We can't put love, justice, or anger in a test tube either. But they're real. Even though we can't prove God from science, there are some things from science that indicate God exists.

(1) The principle of cause and effect

No effect can be produced without a cause. If we go back far enough, we'll eventually come to the uncaused cause—God. This principle is seen in Hebrews 3:4: "For every house is built by some man, but he that built all things is God."

(2) The second law of thermodynamics

According to the law of entropy, the universe is running down. If it's running down, then it's not self-sustaining. If it's not self-sustaining, then it had to have a beginning. If it had a beginning, somebody had to begin it—and you're back to the uncaused Cause. There must be a first cause.

(3) The evidence of design

God's intelligence is revealed in His power. Plants and animals are so constructed that they can appropriate the necessary food, grow, and reproduce. The planets, asteroids, satellites, comets, and meteors are all kept on their courses by gravity. Everything is designed in such a way that it reveals a Designer.

The earth itself has evidence of design. Its distance from the sun is so precise that even a small change would make it either too hot or too cold. The tilt of the earth's axis insures the seasons —and so it goes. Who designed all that?

There is no way to prove God scientifically, but there's much evidence that Someone is in control.

b) From reason

According to Romans 1, man is born with an innate knowledge of God. Man is personal, moral, thinking, and volitional. To say that he came from an amoeba doesn't make sense. Someone had to establish right and wrong, because man has a sense of right and wrong.

Studies by anthropologists show that all men are God-conscious. They have gone all over the world, and everywhere they go they find that people believe in God.

I could go on and on about the scientific evidence and the rational arguments that reveal God, but when you come right down to it, it all boils down to faith. A person finally has to say, "I believe." All the evidence is strictly circumstantial. But once we believe, all of a sudden the proof becomes ours. Hebrews 11:5 says of Enoch, "For before his translation he had this testimony." Where did he have it? In his heart. Romans 8:16 says, "The Spirit himself beareth witness with our spirit, that we are the children of God." When we come to God, all of a sudden the truth is there, because we know Him. No one needs to prove Jesus Christ to me scientifically or rationally.

To please God, you must begin by believing that He is, and that He is the God He claims to be.

II. ENOCH SOUGHT GOD'S REWARD

God "is a rewarder of them that diligently seek him" (Heb. 11:6). It is not enough to believe that God is; we must also believe that God is a moral God and that He rewards the righteous who come to Him. We must recognize that God is personal, loving, and gracious to those who seek Him. Enoch knew that. He didn't believe that God was some great cosmic indifferent primordial cause; he believed that God was a personal, caring, loving God with whom he fellowshiped for three hundred years.

It is not enough to postulate God—like Einstein, who believed that there is definitely a cosmic spirit or force, but that it is impersonal and impossible to know. We can know Him. In fact, in order to please God, we must believe that He is personal, loving, caring, and moral—responding to those who come to Him by rewarding them.

A. The Search

1. 1 Chronicles 28:9b—"If thou seek him, he will be found by thee; but if thou forsake him, he will cast thee off forever."

2. Psalm 58:11a—"Verily, there is a reward for the righteous."

3. Psalm 119:10a—"With my whole heart have I sought thee."

4. Proverbs 8:17—"I love those who love me, and those who seek me early shall find me."

5. Proverbs 11:18b—"To him that soweth righteousness shall be a sure reward."

6. Jeremiah 29:13—"Ye shall seek me, and find me, when ye shall search for me with all your heart."

B. The Specifics

What is the reward for those who seek Him? Matthew 6:33 says, "Seek ye first the kingdom of God, and his righteousness, and all these things shall be added unto you." That means that everything that God could give is our reward. We are joint-heirs with Jesus Christ, and God has promised everything to Him. God gives us forgiveness, a new heart, the Holy Spirit, eternal life, blessings, mercy, grace, peace, joy, love, heaven—everything.

C. The Surety

You may ask, "What if I seek Him, and I ask Him for all that, and He doesn't give it to me?" That doesn't happen.

1. John 6:37b—"Him that cometh to me I will in no wise cast out."

2. Hebrews 7:25a—"Wherefore, he is able also to save them to the uttermost that come unto God by him." Anyone who comes to Him He saves completely.

D. The Standard

To please God you must first believe that He is. Second, you must believe that He is a moral God, that He has righteous standards. You must come on His terms, believing that there's a reward if you do. There's only one way to get there.

1. John 14:6—"Jesus saith unto him, I am the way, the truth, and the life; no man cometh unto the Father, but by me."

2. Acts 4:12—"Neither is there salvation in any other; for there is no other name under heaven given among men, whereby we must be saved."

3. 1 John 2:23—"Whosoever denieth the Son, the same hath not the Father; he that confesseth the Son hath the Father also."

4. 2 John 9—"Whosoever transgresseth and abideth not in the doctrine of Christ, hath not God. He that abideth in the doctrine of Christ, he hath both the Father and the Son."

Enoch pleased God because he believed that God is and because he sought God's reward. God set a standard, and Enoch said, "I'll come to You on the basis of that standard." Jesus says to all people, "Come unto me, all ye that labor and are heavy laden, and I will give you rest" (Matt. 11:28). He gives forgiveness, peace, joy, heaven, and eternal life. There's only one way to come to God, though, and that's by faith in Jesus Christ. If you seek Him with your whole heart you'll find Him.

III. ENOCH WALKED WITH GOD

After a person believes that God is, that He can save him, that he needs the reward He offers, and after he comes to Him on His terms—that's only the beginning. The next thing God wants him to do is to walk with Him. Twice in Genesis 5 it says that "Enoch walked with God" (vv. 22, 24). The phrase "walked with God" is used interchangeably with the phrase "pleased God" in the Septuagint. God was pleased when Enoch walked with Him.

The word *walk* in the New Testament basically refers to the manner of daily conduct. For example, an unbeliever walks according to the things of the world, and a believer walks in the Spirit. Enoch continued daily in the presence of God.

A. Reconciliation

Amos 3:3 asks, "Can two walk together, except they be agreed?" No. Two people walking together in intimate harmony presupposes harmony and agreement. When we say that a man walks with God, that implies the rebellion is over. Every man born into this world is in open rebellion against God. Romans 5:10 says that we were His enemies. But when a man walks with God, the war is over. God's standards are met, and reconciliation takes place.

48

This is illustrated in Ephesians 4:17-19, where Paul shows that the old walk was:

1. Self-centered—"the vanity of their mind"

2. Ignorant—"having the understanding darkened"

3. Dead to God—"being alienated from the life of God"

4. Blind—"the blindness of their heart"

5. Shameless—"being past feeling, have given themselves over unto lasciviousness, to work all uncleanness with greediness"

But in verse 20 Paul says, "But ye have not so learned Christ." Now that we're Christians, we have a new walk. We're no longer cut off from the life of God, living in sin and uncleanness. We're changed—and we're walking with God.

To begin with, a walk with God presupposes reconciliation. We can't begin to walk with God until we've come to the foot of the cross, until our sins have been forgiven, until the rebellion is over, and until we move over to God's side.

B. Corresponding Nature

Do you know anyone who is friends with a goldfish? I don't. You may say, "That's ridiculous. How could you have a goldfish for a friend? What would you do—drag a bowl around?" You're right—it is ridiculous. But do you know what that is like? That is like a sinful man having fellowship with God. God doesn't fellowship with sinners —they live in a different atmosphere. A sinful man is in a whole different world than God is in—he has no corresponding nature. You can't take a goldfish for a walk or sit down in your living room and have a conversation with him. Why? Because you live in two different worlds. You can't talk together in either atmosphere; you can't climb in the bowl and talk to him, and he can't climb out of the bowl and talk to you. The same is true of a sinful man and God. He cannot have fellowship with God on the basis of his own nature because there is no corresponding sphere in which the two of them can be agreed. To walk with God means that there must be a common life. Something must happen to allow a man to step into a domain where he previously couldn't exist.

When we become Christians, our citizenship is no longer on earth; it is in heaven (Phil. 3:20). According to Ephesians, we walk in the heavenlies. Do you know that when we become saved we automatically step into a different sphere? Once this happens, we are able to walk with God. We were goldfish, but God gave us a new nature that is capable of communing with Him. Walking with God presupposes a change in nature. That is what Paul meant when he said, "Therefore, if any man be in Christ, he is a new creation; old things are passed away; behold, all things are become new" (2 Cor. 5:17). We need a new nature to walk with God.

C. Moral Fitness

God does not walk out of the way of holiness. In the Old Testament, before God would walk through the camp of Israel, He always told them to remove everything defiled. God will not walk in any way but the way of holiness. Before Christ commences His walk in the Millennium, all things that offend must be cast out. God keeps no company with the unclean (cf. Hab. 1:13).

The point is this: walking with God requires a holy life. According to 1 John 1:5-10 this involves confession and repentance. The only ones that God ever walks with are those who are continually confessing their sin and being cleansed. The walk with God presupposes a moral fitness or holiness.

D. Surrendered Will

God doesn't force His will on anyone. God only offers Himself. When a man comes to God, he comes because he wills to come. Jesus simply said, "Come" (Matt. 11:28). The end of the book of Revelation says, "Come" (Rev.

22:17). Isaiah, speaking for God, said, "Come" (Isa. 1:18). Jesus, with sorrow in His heart, said, "Ye will not come to me, that ye might have life" (John 5:40). God forces Himself on no one. But when a man comes to God, He demands that all in His company surrender fully to His will. This is a surrender of love. It's not a depressing submissiveness; it's a surrender of love. Second John 6a says, "This is love, that we walk after his commandments." It's love, not bondage.

E. Spiritual Fellowship

The phrase "Enoch walked with God" means that they had a steady, unbroken communion. Do you know how long Enoch walked with God? Three hundred years! If you want to read the account of a great life—in four words—there it is. They had three hundred years of continuous, steady, sweet communion. No wonder Enoch took a walk with God one day and kept right on walking into heaven!

1. Defined

In the New Testament the phrase "walking in the Spirit" is the same thing as walking with God. The Spirit of God is God Himself, and the believer is to walk in the Spirit. This means that we're to move in the atmosphere of the Spirit's presence, continually being bathed in the consciousness of God's presence.

2. Demanded

Galatians 5:25 says, "If we live in the Spirit, let us also walk in the Spirit." According to Romans 8:9 we live in the Spirit; so walking in the Spirit is something we are also to do. What's so important about that? Galatians 5:16 says, "Walk in the Spirit, and ye shall not fulfill the lust of the flesh." And not only that; if we walk in the Spirit, we will have these characteristics in our lives: love, joy, peace, long-suffering, gentleness, goodness, faith, meekness, self-control (Gal. 5:22- 23a). We need to walk in the Spirit.

3. Described

Walking in the Spirit is wonderful. In the New Testament it is described under many different terms. For example, it is described as:

a) A *truthful* walk (3 John 4)

b) An *honest* walk (Rom. 13:13)

c) A *loving* walk (Eph. 5:2)

d) An *enlightened* walk (Eph. 5:8)

e) A *wise* walk (Eph. 5:15)

f) A *good* walk (Eph. 2:10)

g) A *worthy* walk (Eph. 4:1)

4. Demonstrated

You may say, "I'd like to have somebody I could follow. Whom could I look at that walks with God?" You could look at Enoch or Noah—they walked with God. But above all Jesus demonstrated what it was like to walk with God. First John 2:6 says, "He that saith he abideth in him ought himself also to walk, even as he [Christ] walked." Christ is our example. If you want to know how to walk with God, just look at Jesus—He was always in communion with the Father.

Above all these facets of walking in the Spirit, our walk is to be a walk of faith. Second Corinthians 5:7 says, "For we walk by faith, not by sight." Colossians 2:6 says, "As ye have, therefore, received Christ Jesus the Lord, so walk ye in him." How did you receive Him? By faith. So, how do you walk? By faith. Enoch believed God. He never saw Him, but he believed in Him.

IV. ENOCH PREACHED FOR GOD

Enoch not only walked with God, he affected everybody around him. In Jude 14-15 we find Enoch preaching for God:

"Enoch also, the seventh from Adam, prophesied of these [referring back to false teachers], saying, Behold, the Lord cometh with ten thousands of his saints, to execute judgment upon all, and to convict all that are ungodly among them of all their ungodly deeds which they have ungodly committed, and of all their hard speeches which ungodly sinners have spoken against him."

Jude is speaking of false teachers that will be judged. So to prove how much God hates them—and how much He's always hated them—he pulls out a prophecy that God gave to Enoch, the seventh man from Adam. Even that far back God hated false teachers.

Someone may ask, "What was Enoch preaching about? Look when he lived—only seven generations from the first man on earth. It couldn't have been that bad." It was in fact an evil generation. The Cainite civilization was already corrupted, and it was difficult to walk with God. Enoch was in the midst of a polluted society, but he preached to the ungodly and let them know that God was going to judge them.

I believe God was pleased with Enoch because his faith wasn't just something that he felt in his heart. His faith was active; he was fearless; he confronted the ungodly—and he did it by faith. He preached the judgment of God on sinners because God told him to preach it. He believed it would happen, so he preached it by faith.

V. ENOCH ENTERED GOD'S PRESENCE

Genesis 5:24 says, "Enoch walked with God, and he was not; for God took him." Hebrews 11:5 says, "By faith Enoch was translated [lit., "crossed over"] that he should not see death, and was not found, because God had translated him; for before his translation he had this testimony, that he pleased God."

Some commentators say that God took Enoch because He didn't want him to ever get polluted by the corruptions of the world. Enoch had been so faithful for many years that God saw there was no sense in leaving him in the world—and He took him up. Also, I believe God took him up because He loved him. Did you know that God enjoys the fellowship of

His saints? Psalm 116:15 says, "Precious in the sight of the Lord is the death of his saints." Why is it so precious? Because God loves His saints. In Enoch's case, he didn't die, but he was certainly precious to God.

Enoch is a wonderful picture of the believers who will be alive on the earth when our Lord descends in the air to catch up His bride with a shout (1 Thess. 4:16-17). Just as Enoch was translated to heaven without seeing death, so also will those of God's people who are alive at the rapture. This ancient picture of the rapture shows that God has the prerogative over death.

Do you want to please God? Do you believe that God *is*? Do you believe that He rewards those who come to Him on His terms? Have you committed your life to walk with Him? Have you opened your mouth to speak for Him? If so, the time will come when you'll enter His presence. That pleases Him most of all.

Focusing on the Facts

1. What place do works have in the Christian life (see p. 40)?
2. How does the life of faith begin (see p. 41)?
3. Why was God pleased with Enoch (see p. 42)?
4. The only way God can be known is by _____, not _____ (see p. 43).
5. Does the fact that God's existence can't be discovered using the scientific method prove that He doesn't exist? Explain (see pp. 44-45).
6. What reward does God promise for those who seek Him (see p. 47)?
7. True or false: God will never turn away those who come to Him with genuine faith (see p. 47).
8. True or false: It is possible for someone who doesn't believe in Jesus Christ to please God (see pp. 47-48).
9. What is meant by the word *walk* in the New Testament (see p. 48)?
10. What must take place before we can walk with God (see pp. 48-49)?
11. Why can't sinful men have fellowship with God (see pp. 49-50)?

12. Walking with God requires a _____ _____ (see p. 50).
13. Describe what it means to walk in the Spirit (see p. 52).
14. What message did Enoch preach (see p. 53)?
15. What are some of the reasons God took Enoch into His presence (see p. 53)?

Pondering the Principles

1. Enoch is commended for his exemplary walk with God. As Christians, we too should be examples to the world of what it means to walk with God. We walk with Him by walking in the Spirit (Gal. 5:25), through studying His Word, by submitting to the Spirit's leading, and by confessing our sins. How is your walk in the Spirit progressing? Galatians 5:22-23 lists nine characteristics that the Spirit produces in our lives as we walk in the Spirit. Take a few moments and measure your life against those standards. The extent to which your life manifests those characteristics is the extent to which you are walking in the Spirit.

2. Jude tells us that Enoch confronted the false teaching and ungodliness of his day. We too live in an ungodly society saturated with false teaching. Like Enoch we are responsible to confront it, both with our lives (Phil. 2:15) and our words (2 Tim. 2:24-26). Make the commitment to live a life-style that will be a rebuke to false teaching, then confront false doctrine when the opportunity arises.

4

Noah and the Obedience of Faith

Outline

Introduction
A. The Proof of Faith
B. The Progress of Faith

Lesson
 I. Noah Responded to God's Word (v. 7a)
    A. His Commitment
    B. His Care
    C. His Challenge
II. Noah Rebuked the World (v. 7b)
    A. The Sermon
    B. The Society
       1. Wicked
       2. Grievous to God
       3. Demon possessed
       4. Corrupt
    C. The Sentencing
       1. His purpose
       2. His patience
    D. The Similarities
III. Noah Received God's Righteousness (v. 7c)

Introduction

A. The Proof of Faith

In Hebrews 11 we are given great examples of faith. In each case genuine faith was demonstrated by something the individual did. Faith in itself is such a fragile commodity that its only visibility comes in the works and deeds that are done. For example, if I say that I believe in God, you cannot verify the genuineness of my faith unless you see something that indicates that I do (cf. James 2:17). In Hebrews 11 we find that the heroes of faith are all tied together by something they did in their lives that showed that they genuinely believed God.

B. The Progress of Faith

The Holy Spirit begins the illustrations of faith with Abel (v. 4) and discusses the entrance into the life of faith—the beginning. Second, He moves into a discussion of Enoch (vv. 5-6) and the walk of faith—the continuance. Third, He comes to Noah (v. 7), who illustrates the work of faith—the obedience.

There is a progression. The record of Abel is of one who worshiped God. The record of Enoch shows us one who worshiped and walked with God. And in Noah we see one who worshiped God, walked with God, and worked for God. Noah takes faith a step further. It's interesting that faith works this way—that worship is required before a walk can take place, and that a walk must be present before one can have the work of faith. That is how God has established it. Some people only get as far as the first step—they come to God by faith. Some get to the second step and walk with God for a while. And then there are people who are like Noah, who not only believe God and walk with Him but are committed to continuing. That's the obedience of faith.

Noah's faith was remarkable. It was so far beyond human rationale that it doesn't make sense to the normal mind. Unless a man knew God and had spiritual insight, he would be a fool to do what Noah did. The fact that Noah did what God told him to do, even though he couldn't see anything past his own trust, is absolutely stupendous. He believed God to the point that he did what seemed totally irrational.

There are three great proofs in Hebrews 11:7 that tell us Noah's faith was legitimate: (1) he responded to God's word; (2) he rebuked the world; and (3) he received God's righteousness. Those are three classic indications of true faith. Somebody whose faith is real will respond to God's Word, live as a rebuke to the world, and receive God's righteousness, which comes to those who believe.

Lesson

I. NOAH RESPONDED TO GOD'S WORD (v. 7a)

"By faith Noah, being warned of God of things not seen as yet, moved with fear, prepared an ark, to the saving of his house."

A. His Commitment

Noah believed God so much that he built an ark. To do so may have appeared on the surface to be foolhardy. Imagine the laughing and jeering from his neighbors as he was building. But God told Noah, "Judgment is coming. I am going to destroy the world by water. You'd better build a boat." Noah spent more than a hundred years building a boat somewhere in Mesopotamia between the Tigris and Euphrates rivers, miles and miles from any ocean. After seventy or eighty years I would have begun to wonder. But Noah exhibited faith that responded to God's word. True faith doesn't question its obedience.

Noah was no different that we are. He must have had many tasks that occupied his time. Giving up a long period of time to build a boat took great commitment. In fact, Noah likely never understood much about boats, because he didn't live in an area where there were seagoing ships. But he listened to God and spent his life obeying what God said.

B. His Care

Verse 7 says, "By faith Noah, being warned of God . . ." The phrase "of God" should be included because it's obvious that it was God who spoke. The phrase "warned of God of things not seen as yet" shows Noah's test of faith.

Hebrews 11:1 says, "Faith is the substance of things hoped for, the evidence of things not seen."

Verse 7 says that "Noah . . . moved with fear." You may say, "Aha! That's why he did it. God held a big stick over him and said, 'You'd better do this, or I'll let you have it!' " That isn't what that means. The word *fear* may give you the impression that Noah acted under the influence of fright, but the Greek word means "to reverence." Noah did what God told him to do because he reverenced God's word. He acted with pious care. He treated the message of God with great reverence and prepared the ark. Noah's faith was honored, and his house was saved. Eight souls were saved: his wife, his three sons—Shem, Ham, and Japheth—and his sons' three wives.

C. His Challenge

We'll look at this incident in Genesis 6 to see some of the fascinating things that took place.

1. Verse 14—God said to Noah, "Make thee an ark of gopher wood; rooms shalt thou make in the ark; and shalt pitch it within and without with pitch." That was a challenge to faith on an absolutely unprecedented scale. What would you do if God told you to build a gigantic ship in the middle of the wilderness? One of the greatest acts of faith in the history of the world occurred when Noah began chopping down that first tree.

2. Verse 15—This was God's verbal blueprint for the ark: "The length of the ark shall be three hundred cubits, the breadth of it fifty cubits, and the height of it thirty cubits." There's disagreement as to how long a cubit was, but it ranged from 17.5 inches to 22 inches. Using the lowest measurement, the ark was 437.5 feet long, 72.92 feet wide, and 43.75 feet high (about the height of a four-story building). Since the ark had three decks (see v. 16), it had a total deck area of approximately 95,700 square feet (more than 20 standard basketball courts), with a volume of 1,396,000 cubic feet. That's a big ship. Its size puts it in the category of the oceangoing vessels of today. From what we can tell, it was like a large covered raft, rectangular and flat-bottomed.

For centuries people built ships in various proportions; but once British naval machinists found the formula for the dimensions of the battleship *Dreadnought* at the turn of the century, all naval construction followed its proportions, and it became a standard. The dimensions for *Dreadnought* are quite similar to those of the ark!

3. Verse 17—"Behold, I, even I, do bring a flood of waters upon the earth, to destroy all flesh, wherein is the breath of life, from under heaven; and everything that is in the earth shall die." God told Noah that it was going to rain and that He was going to bring a flood of waters upon the earth. That was not an easy thing for Noah to believe—especially since Noah didn't know what rain was.

   Genesis 2:6 says, "There went up a mist from the earth, and watered the whole face of the ground." The earth was watered by a mist coming up from the ground. Perhaps the earth was also covered by a mist (cf. Gen. 1:6-7). A mist surrounding the earth could explain why people lived so long before the Flood. If the sun's rays never penetrated the mist, people would have been protected from the deterioration process brought about by the sun's rays. But when God broke up the fountains of the great deep with the Flood (Gen. 7:11), the whole atmosphere of the earth was changed, and man's life was immediately shortened because of the penetrating rays of the sun.

   There are a number of reasons why human reason was completely opposed to what God had revealed to Noah.

   a) Since there had never been any rain, who would have expected a flood?

   b) It seemed unlikely that God would destroy the whole human race, with His mercy swallowed up by His justice.

   c) The judgment was a long way off—120 years away (Gen. 6:3)—and Noah could have rationalized and said, "That gives people a lot of time to repent and reform. They'll probably shape up by then."

d) When Noah preached, no one believed his message. After 120 years of preaching without any results, one might begin to doubt the message. But Noah kept on preaching.

e) Noah must have endured mocking and scoffing from his neighbors and the townspeople.

f) Noah might have asked, "Even if the flood comes, how would such a vessel float—especially when it's loaded down with two of every kind of animal?"

g) Also, the ark had no anchor, no mast, no steering, no rudder, no sail—and Noah didn't know anything about sailing, anyway.

Against all that, Noah believed God.

4. Verse 18—"But with thee will I establish my covenant." God in effect said, "Noah, I'm not going to destroy everybody. I'm going to maintain My promise to you." What was this promise based on? Verse 8: "But Noah found grace in the eyes of the Lord." And according to verse 9, Noah was a just man, perfect in his generation, and he walked with God. The rest of the world was to be drowned, but Noah found grace in the eyes of the Lord.

Noah didn't have grace in himself; the grace was in the eyes of the Lord. God gives grace to whom He will. Nothing in a sinner can appeal to God. Noah was no different than any other son of Adam (cf. Gen. 9:21-22). If the grace of God had not restrained sin in his heart, he would have been as wicked as the rest. It is God's right to give His grace to whom He will. God spared Noah and made a covenant with him.

5. Verses 19-21—"Of every living thing of all flesh, two of every sort shalt thou bring into the ark, to keep them alive with thee; they shall be male and female. Of fowls after their kind, and of cattle after their kind, of every creeping thing of the earth after its kind, two of every sort shall come unto thee, to keep them alive. And take

thou unto thee of all food that is eaten, and thou shalt gather it to thee; and it shall be for food for thee, and for them." God said to Noah, "After you've built the boat, I want you to get the animals into it." Can you imagine the scene? Noah waited at the door while these animals came from everywhere. There is no way to explain this phenomenon other than that God Himself herded them into the ark.

Someone has calculated that the ark, from a spatial standpoint, could easily handle several thousand animals. That doesn't mean that two of every animal in the world was in the ark. There are animals, and then there are kinds of animals. The kinds can diversify until there is a tremendous variety, but it is still the same kind, and each animal within it can be traced to a common ancestor.

There wouldn't have been any problem housing the animals, but this still was a strange command. How were the animals going to arrive? How would they live together? How would they be fed? Who would keep the ark clean? They were to be in the ark for almost a year. Noah received a command that staggered the imagination; but he was a man of faith, and he began to build.

6. Verse 22—"Thus did Noah; according to all that God commanded him, so did he." Noah was a man of amazing faith. He came by faith to God, he walked by faith with God, and now he was obeying God in faith—even though it staggered his imagination to conceive of what God had asked him to do. He believed God, and he believed what God said would happen. Many of us run out of patience with God in a week, but Noah believed God's promise for 120 years!

What was the ground of the faith that Noah exhibited? God's word. He believed that God meant what He said, and he obeyed God. He believed God's word and treated it with reverence. Noah believed God's word about judgment, about promise—about everything. He built the ark as it was supposed to be built, and he obeyed God to the letter.

63

Nineteenth-century English preacher C. H. Spurgeon said in a sermon on the fearfulness of future judgment that he who does not believe that God will punish sin, will not believe that He will pardon it through atoning blood. There are some people who want to believe God about His promises but don't want to believe Him about judgment. Noah believed Him about both. Spurgeon pleaded with believers not to be unbelieving with regard to the terrible threatenings of God to the ungodly, because the act of disbelieving God at one point drives us to disbelieve Him upon other points of revealed truth. Noah not only believed that he was going to receive a promise, but he also believed that the whole world was going to be destroyed.

II. NOAH REBUKED THE WORLD (v. 7b)

"By faith Noah, being warned of God of things not seen as yet, moved with fear, prepared an ark to the saving of his house, by which he condemned the world."

A. The Sermon

Did you know that Noah was a preacher? Do you know what he preached? Second Peter 2:4-5a says, "God spared not the angels that sinned, but cast them down to hell, and delivered them into chains of darkness, to be reserved unto judgment; and spared not the old world, but saved Noah, the eighth person, a preacher of righteousness." What was his sermon? His sermon was 120 years building a boat. Every time people saw him working on the ark, or heard him chop down a tree, or saw him walking with lumber, they heard his sermon: "Judgment is coming; judgment is coming; judgment is coming." He preached his sermon with his life. Every chopped tree, every sawed plank, and every driven spike preached a sermon that said, "Judgment is coming. Believe God for refuge." For 120 years he preached his sermon, but there was no response. Noah rejected discouragement and by faith went on as a living rebuke to his world. He rebuked his world because he was a man of faith. Because the world doesn't believe God, a person who does rebukes the world just by believing Him.

B. The Society

Genesis 6 provides some characteristics of the society in which Noah lived.

1. Wicked

Verse 5 says, "God saw that the wickedness of man was great in the earth, and that every imagination of the thoughts of his heart was only evil continually." Human eyes can see the wicked actions of man, but only God can tell what goes on in his heart (cf. Ezek. 11:5). Not only were his deeds evil, but he was vile on the inside.

2. Grievous to God

Verse 6 says, "It repented the Lord that he had made man on the earth, and it grieved him at his heart." God is neither taken by surprise, nor does He change His mind. We have an anthropomorphism here—a statement about God in human terms. From a human standpoint, it appeared as if God repented. First Samuel 15:29 says, "The Glory of Israel [a name for God] will not lie or change his mind; for he is not a man that he should change his mind" (NASB). From God's perspective nothing changed; but from a human perspective it appeared as though God had changed His plan and decided to destroy mankind.

Notice that it was not only His justice that was offended, but His heart was grieved. God is a personal, feeling God.

3. Demon possessed

Verse 7 says, "The Lord said, I will destroy man whom I have created from the face of the earth; both man, and beast, and the creeping thing, and the fowls of the air; for it repenteth me that I have made them." What a terrible resolution! The race was largely demon possessed and was so corrupted that men, women, and children had to be destroyed. I believe that the sons of God who came down and cohabited with the daughters of men were none other than fallen angels—demons (cf. vv. 1-4). God had to destroy that generation.

4. Corrupt

Verse 12 says, "God looked upon the earth, and, behold, it was corrupt; for all flesh had corrupted his way upon the earth." The fact that they had corrupted His way shows that they knew what His way was but chose to go their own way. Romans 1:21 says, "When they knew God, they glorified him not as God, neither were thankful, but became vain in their imaginations, and their foolish heart was darkened." Verse 25 says that they "exchanged the truth of God for a lie, and worshiped and served the creature more than the Creator." They turned their backs on God and corrupted His way. Before you impugn God remember that God gave them every chance; but they went their own way.

C. The Sentencing

In Genesis 6:13 God discloses His sentence of destruction to Noah: "God said unto Noah, The end of all flesh is come before me; for the earth is filled with violence through them; and, behold, I will destroy them with the earth." The world was corrupt and rotten, and everyone was going his own way. God told Noah that He was going to destroy them. It's interesting that throughout the Bible God tells His special people about coming judgment. Amos 3:7 says, "Surely the Lord God does nothing, unless He reveals His secret counsel to His servants, the prophets" (NASB). God inevitably tells someone that His judgment is coming, and He does so here with Noah.

1. His purpose

Someone might say, "It still appears to me that God is awfully hardened to come down and wipe out the whole world. It seems His mercy ran out, and His justice overwhelmed Him." That isn't true. The fact that God's time of patience will end and that He will strike out in justice is the only hope for a sin-cursed world. If God doesn't act to destroy, then we face an eternity of sinfulness. The fact that Jesus is going to come in judgment is our hope as Christians, because if sin is not judged, we will live eternally in a sinful and vile world. God is holy and just, and He will destroy sin. He has already destroyed our sin as believers in Christ. Don't believe that there isn't mercy and grace in destruction and judgment. Pastor Donald Grey Barnhouse said that hell is as much a part of the love story of God as is heaven.

2. His patience

God's judgment is slow and patient. Genesis 5:21 says, "Enoch lived sixty and five years and begot Methuselah." What's the significance of Methuselah? His name is significant. It means "when he is dead, it shall be sent." In his name is a divine revelation. It was as though God said to Enoch, "You see that baby you just had? The world will last as long as he lives. When he is dead, then it shall be sent." What shall be sent? The great Flood. The world was to last as long as the son of Enoch lived.

First Peter 3:20 says, "The longsuffering of God waited in the days of Noah." What was God waiting for (besides waiting for Noah to build the ark)? He was waiting for Methuselah to die. By Methuselah's very name, God was saying that He wouldn't send judgment until he died. How long did Methuselah live? Longer than any man in the history of the world—969 years. That tells you something about the grace of God. Before you impugn the justice of God, look again. God was so merciful that He waited almost a thousand years for mankind to change. But they only went further and further away.

Did the People of Noah's Day Really Have a Chance to Know the Truth?

Some might argue that the world never knew the truth. But that isn't so.

1. Romans 1:19-20 says that men have enough knowledge of God in the visible creation to be without excuse.

2. They had the revelation of a Redeemer in Genesis 3:15—the promised Seed of the woman to bruise the serpent's head.

3. The institution of the expiatory sacrifice as the way to approach God was given during the time of Abel (Gen. 4:4). They knew how to come to God (cf. Gen. 8:20).

4. The mark placed on Cain was a constant reminder of how God viewed sin.

5. Adam lived 930 years and probably spent much of that time telling men the truth about what sin brought him.

6. The preaching of Enoch was warning (Jude 14-15).

7. The preaching of Noah was warning (see pp. 52-53).

8. The Holy Spirit was striving with men (Gen. 6:3).

Don't say that Noah's generation didn't know. They knew—they just became hardened and rejected the truth.

D. The Similarities

Matthew 24:37 says, "As the days of Noah were, so shall also the coming of the Son of man be." What were the characteristics of Noah's day? Are they repeated today?

1. In Noah's day they laughed at the preaching of the gospel. They still do today.

2. In Noah's day there was a multiplication of people (cf. Gen. 6:1). Some say that is duplicated today in the population explosion.

3. In Noah's day God dealt patiently with a sinful world. God is still dealing patiently in grace today.

4. In Noah's day God had His own preachers. God still uses His preachers today.

5. In Noah's day God's Spirit strove with man. Yet God said, "My Spirit shall not always strive with man" (Gen.

6:3*a*). With the striving was a threat of the Spirit's removal. The Spirit is striving with man today, but 2 Thessalonians 2:6-7 promises that the Spirit of God, the Restrainer, shall be taken away.

6. In Noah's day God's message was rejected. It still is today.

7. In Noah's day there was a remnant who found grace. There still is today.

8. In Noah's day Enoch was miraculously translated. Today we look forward to the rapture of the believers before judgment.

9. In Noah's day there was demon activity on the earth. There still is today.

Noah was a man of faith. We know his faith was real because he responded to God's word and rebuked the world.

III. NOAH RECEIVED GOD'S RIGHTEOUSNESS (v. 7*c*)

"Noah . . . became heir of the righteousness which is by faith."

Noah was the first man in the Bible to be called righteous. In Genesis 6:9 he is called "a just man." The Greek translation of the Old Testament, the Septuagint, uses the word *dikaios* to describe Noah, which means "righteous." The only way to receive the righteousness of God is by faith. If Noah became the heir of righteousness, and the only way to get righteousness is by faith, he must have been a man of faith. The third way, then, that we know Noah was a man of faith was that he was declared righteous.

Noah illustrates the life, the walk, and the work of faith. He is a model of faith. God needs more men and women like Noah who believe God and obey Him no matter how strange and difficult the command might be. I pray that God will help us to obey His Word—no matter how difficult—to stand as a rebuke to a corrupt world, and to be that which establishes us as righteous in His sight.

Focusing on the Facts

1. How is faith made visible in a person's life (see p. 58)?
2. In what way was Noah's faith made evident (see p. 59)?
3. True or false: Noah built the ark because he was afraid of what God might do to him if he didn't (see p. 60).
4. What is one possible reason that people lived longer before the Flood (see p. 61)?
5. Describe some of the factors that made it difficult for Noah to believe there would be a flood (see pp. 61-62).
6. True or false: God's covenant with Noah was based on Noah's good works (see p. 62).
7. What was the basis of Noah's faith (see pp. 63-64)?
8. What was the content of the message Noah preached (see p. 64)?
9. Did God change His mind about having created the human race? Explain (see p. 65).
10. Why is the fact that Jesus will return to earth in judgment our hope as Christians (see pp. 66-67)?
11. In what way was Methuselah a manifestation of the grace of God (see p. 67)?
12. How would you respond to someone who claimed that God didn't give fair warning to the people of Noah's day before sending the Flood (see pp. 67-68)?
13. True or false: Noah was the first man in the Bible to be called righteous (see p. 69).

Pondering the Principles

1. Noah not only believed that judgment was coming but also put his faith into practice by building an ark. We often say we believe God—as long as He doesn't put us in a position where we have to trust Him! As you study Hebrews 11 ask yourself how all the people named there put their faith in God into practice. Then ask God to show you concrete ways in which you can put your faith into practice.

2. It was 120 years from the time God warned Noah that the Flood was coming until it came. It would have been easy for Noah to have given up during that time, but he didn't—he persevered in his faith. Have you been waiting on the Lord for something for

so long that your faith is beginning to waver? Perhaps you are involved in a ministry that has borne little fruit. Or maybe you've been praying for someone's salvation for many years, and he seems no closer to God than when you began. If you are tempted to give up, remember Noah's patient faith, and memorize Hebrews 10:23 this week: "Let us hold fast the profession of our faith without wavering (for he is faithful [who] promised)."

5
The Faith of Abraham

Outline

Introduction

Lesson
I. The Pilgrimage of Faith (v. 8)
   A. His Submission to God
   B. His Sovereign Call
   C. His Separation from the World
II. The Patience of Faith (vv. 9-10)
   A. The Pattern
      1. Abraham's transience
      2. Abraham's test
   B. The Passages
      1. 2 Thessalonians 1:4
      2. Hebrews 12:1
      3. James 1:3-4
      4. James 5:7-8, 11
   C. The Perspective
      1. Ezekiel 48:35b
      2. Colossians 3:2
      3. Genesis 13:12
      4. 2 Timothy 2:3-4a
      5. Hebrews 11:27
      6. Hebrews 12:1b-2a
III. The Power of Faith (vv. 11-12)
   A. Matthew 19:26
   B. Mark 9:23
   C. Luke 18:27
   D. Matthew 17:19-20
   E. Philippians 4:13
   F. Ephesians 3:20

Introduction

Christians live by faith. We base our lives on what we've never seen. We've never seen God, Jesus Christ, the Holy Spirit, heaven, or hell. We've never seen any of the men who wrote the Bible. We've never seen an original manuscript of the Bible. We've never seen any of the graces that God says He dispenses to us, since they are not tangible or visible to the human eye. Yet we bank our lives and our eternal destiny on things that we have never seen. The life of faith has some specific ingredients that I believe are pointed out explicitly in this particular text as we look at Abraham. Hebrews 11:8-19 presents Abraham as a pattern for faith.

Abraham's life was characterized by faith. Genesis 15:6 says, "He [Abraham] believed in the Lord; and he [God] counted it to him for righteousness." Abraham was declared righteous because of his faith. All through his life he acted on faith. He is a pattern.

There are five features of faith in this passage that show us the complete pattern: the pilgrimage of faith, the patience of faith, the power of faith, the positivism of faith, and the proof of faith. And since Abraham is a spiritual prototype of every man of faith, we're going to consider this narrative in its spiritual sense—the sense in which I believe the writer of Hebrews wanted us to consider it. These five features, then, are the standards for faith.

Lesson

I. THE PILGRIMAGE OF FAITH (v. 8)

"By faith Abraham, when he was called to go out into a place which he should after receive for an inheritance, obeyed; and he went out, not knowing where he went."

If someone told us that he was going somewhere, but he didn't know where, we'd consider him to be in danger of getting into trouble. Why? Because he hadn't carefully charted his course. God in effect told Abraham, "Get up and get out of this city. I'm going to use you to establish a nation. You're going to be the father of a nation, and through you all the families of the earth will be blessed." It was through Abraham's loins that the Messiah came, and it is in the Messiah that all the world is blessed. God said, "Abraham, get up and go to a land that I'll show you." That is recorded in Genesis 12-18.

A. His Submission to God

The phrase "when he was called" in verse 8 is a present participle in the Greek and speaks of action going on at the same time as that of the leading verb, which in this verse is "obeyed." In other words, the verse could read, "Abraham, while he was being called, obeyed." Abraham immediately obeyed God's call.

Verse 8 says, "He went out, not knowing where he went." The word *knowing* is the Greek word *epistamai* and means "to fix one's attention on, to put one's thoughts on." The end of the verse, then, reads, "He went out, not even putting his thoughts on where he was going." He was so obedient that he didn't even think about where he was going. He was saying, "God, You said go, so I'll go. Where I go is immaterial." It was a question of obedience. That's the pilgrimage of faith.

B. His Sovereign Call

Abraham lived in an unregenerate world. He was from the city of Ur, which was located in Chaldea, or southern Mesopotamia, between the Tigris and Euphrates rivers. It was a fertile land, where the Garden of Eden was originally located and where the great city of Babylon was eventually built. Abraham grew up in a pagan home. Joshua 24:2 says, "Terah, the father of Abraham . . . served other gods." Abraham lived in an idolatrous, vile culture of paganism. Yet the God of glory condescended in sovereignty to choose Abraham and establish a nation through his loins. Abraham responded with faith and went even while he was being called, and God declared him to be righteous. His pilgrimage of faith led him to forsake his birthplace, his home, his estate. He severed family ties, left loved ones, and abandoned his present habits for future uncertainty. It must have been difficult—but he did it.

C. His Separation from the World

I believe that the life of faith begins with a break from the idolatrous system in which an individual has lived all his life. When a person comes to Jesus Christ, I believe there's a pilgrimage that God demands at that point: to leave the life-style he's been involved in and come into a new kind of life. Abraham's faith separated him from that which was pagan. Salvation demands separation. Practical separation from the world is the beginning of the life of faith. One says, "All right, God. I don't know what You're going to do with me, but I'm going to leave the system of the world and go where You lead me." That's the pilgrimage of faith —the beginning of the life of faith.

There are many passages that deal with the Christian's responsibility to separate himself from the world's system.

1. Romans 12:1-2a—"I beseech you therefore, brethren, by the mercies of God, that ye present your bodies a living sacrifice, holy, acceptable unto God, which is your reasonable service. And be not conformed to this world, but be ye transformed by the renewing of your mind."

2. 2 Corinthians 6:14-16a—"Be ye not unequally yoked together with unbelievers; for what fellowship hath righteousness with unrighteousness? And what communion hath light with darkness? And what concord hath Christ with Belial [Satan]? Or what part hath he that

believeth with an infidel [atheist or unbeliever]? And what agreement hath the temple of God with idols? For ye are the temple of the living God." A theological foundation is given—light and darkness don't mix. Then a practical exhortation is given—don't try to make them mix.

3. Galatians 1:3-4—"Grace be to you, and peace, from God the Father, and from our Lord Jesus Christ, who gave himself for our sins, that he might deliver us from this present evil age." Salvation is to take us out of the system and send us on a pilgrimage, by faith, into a lifestyle we've never known before. That is a problem for many people. I've heard people say, "I don't want to become a Christian because I will have to give up all the things I like to do." Then when they're told that Christians love God, strive to be holy and sinless, desire to read the Bible and go to church, and so on, they often reply, "Oh, what a bore!" That's a common reaction. What they don't understand is that once they become Christians all the things that used to be valuable become worthless, and all the things that used to be worthless are valuable. Why? Because they're different.

4. Hebrews 13:13-14—"Let us go forth, therefore, unto him outside the camp, bearing his reproach." You have to be willing to pay the price, walk away from the system, and go where Jesus went. Verse 14 says, "For here have we no continuing city, but we seek one to come." We're strangers and pilgrims; we don't belong here. Don't get involved with the world's system—go with Jesus outside the system.

5. James 1:27—"Pure religion and undefiled before God and the Father is this: to visit the fatherless and widows in their affliction, and to keep oneself unspotted from the world." That's pure religion.

6. James 4:4—"Ye adulterers and adulteresses, know ye not that the friendship of the world is enmity with God? Whosoever, therefore, will be a friend of the world is the enemy of God."

7. 1 Peter 1:14-15—"As obedient children, not fashioning yourselves according to the former lusts in your ignorance." In other words, "You used to be ignorant, and you didn't know what else to do but lust, but now that you've come to Christ stop doing it!" Verse 15 continues, "But, as he who hath called you is holy, so be ye holy in all manner of life." To be holy means to be separated.

8. 1 Peter 4:1-2—"Forasmuch, then, as Christ hath suffered for us in the flesh, arm yourselves likewise with the same mind; for he that hath suffered in the flesh hath ceased from sin, that he no longer should live the rest of his time in the flesh to the lusts of men but to the will of God."

9. 2 Peter 1:4—"By which are given unto us exceedingly great and precious promises, that by these ye might be partakers of the divine nature, having escaped the corruption that is in the world through lust."

That is basic. At salvation, separation is to occur.

What Is Worldliness?

Is playing cards worldly? The Bible doesn't say that. Is drinking wine worldly? The Bible doesn't say that. Is going to movies worldly? The Bible doesn't say that. You may ask, "Are there any principles that apply to all those things? What is worldliness?" Worldliness is sometimes an act, but most of the time it's an attitude. It's not so much what you do—it's what you want to do.

Worldly people can be restrained from doing worldly things—but it doesn't change the fact that they are worldly. They can be restrained by:

1. Position—Some people are restrained from worldly deeds because they're in a position of responsibility where all eyes are focused on them. But if they knew that nobody would see them, they would do them.

2. Self-imposed legalism—Many people are restrained by a self-imposed legalism that binds them to a system they hate. These

people become the worst kind of pharisaical hypocrites imaginable because they not only have a masquerade of holiness but they also feel guilty for wanting to do what they know they can't.

3. Group pressure—This can happen, for example, to someone who is going to church or attending a Bible study where everybody in the group is studying the Bible and talking about spiritual things—and he wears the mask and plays along. But deep down in his heart he's saying, "I can't take this anymore. I have to get out of here and live it up." That's worldliness.

First John 2:15 says, "Love not the world, neither the things that are in the world." First Timothy 6:10a says, "For the *love* of money is the root of all evil" (emphasis added). Money isn't evil; it's the love of it that is. Worldliness is an attitude. It isn't what you do; it's what you *want* to do.

As a Christian grows he begins to lose his desire to do worldly things. Spiritual maturation is the process of getting to the place where you not only don't do it, but you don't want to do it. The pilgrimage of faith begins by separating yourself. And as you concentrate on Jesus Christ and begin to grow, you will lose your worldly desires.

You can measure your Christian maturity when you find yourself able to do what you want to do. A young Christian may say, "I like to do that, but I can't because I'm a Christian now." As a Christian matures he finds that all the things he wants to do are the things he can do. When this happens, he reaches the level where God is not only controlling the pattern of his living, but He's controlling the pattern of his thinking and desires. That's when the Christian life becomes exciting.

II. THE PATIENCE OF FAITH (vv. 9-10)

A. The Pattern

1. Abraham's transience

Hebrews 11:9 says, "By faith he [Abraham] sojourned." Abraham lived a transient life. The word *sojourned* is the Greek verb *paroikeō*, which is from *oikeō* ("to dwell") and *para* ("alongside"). *Paroikeō* means "to dwell alongside, beside, or among." Verse 9, then, could read, "By faith he dwelt in the land of promise, as in a foreign country, dwelling in tents with Isaac and Jacob, the heirs with him of the same promise."

Even after Abraham reached the land of promise he never got the promise. Abraham never owned the land. God never gave it to him. He did buy a burial plot, which was called Machpelah, but that was all. He was a transient in the land. He had to be patient. He could have said, "Well, God, You brought me over here. I separated myself from my old life, and You told me that I was really going to have a great time. But this is ridiculous—bouncing around from place to place in a tent."

We're much like Abraham. God pulled us out of the world and told us He had something better for us—but we're still waiting for it. We haven't arrived in heaven yet, and like Abraham our pilgrimage through this world can be rough. We need to exhibit what Abraham exhibited—the patience of faith.

In Acts 7:5, Stephen says about Abraham, "And he [God] gave him no inheritance in it [the land], no, not so much as to set his foot on; yet he promised that he would give it to him for a possession, and to his seed after him, when as yet he had no child." When God promised the land to his descendants, Abraham had no children. He had to be patient.

Do You See Yourself as a Pilgrim in This World?

Hebrews 11:9 says that Abraham "sojourned in the land of promise." The Greek word for "sojourned" is *paroikeō*, which literally means "to dwell alongside, beside, or among." This word came to refer to a foreigner who was dwelling in the land without the rights of citizenship. Abraham was a foreigner in the land.

Abraham is a perfect picture of a Christian. Christians are pilgrims on this earth, strangers in this world. We shouldn't invest too much here. Jesus said, "Lay not up for yourselves treasures upon earth, where moth and rust doth corrupt, and where thieves break through and steal, but lay up for yourselves treasures in heaven, where neither moth nor rust doth corrupt, and where thieves do not break through nor steal; for where your treasure is, there will your heart be also" (Matt. 6:19-21). As long as you're only a pilgrim here, just be patient and don't invest too much in this world.

It is better to spend time teaching your son Christian values than it is to make extra money for your bank account. It is better to spend time teaching your daughter about Jesus than it is to shop for the latest fashions. Order your priorities. Work for the real rewards.

2. Abraham's test

Although Abraham waited patiently for the valuable things and remained faithful, he never saw God's promise fulfilled.

The hardest times are the in-between times. I imagine that when Abraham first left Ur he was excited. The time spent in the presence of God must have been tremendous. But it was the time in-between that must have been difficult. The real test of the patience of faith is to work, to wait, and to watch—even when you can't see what's happening. Unfortunately, many Christians become weary and give up.

If we knew that the Lord was coming next Saturday, many of us would work hard because we'd know it would be over Saturday. But when believers start looking at life like that, they've lost the patience of faith. We need to take it a day at a time and believe God.

The patience of faith is illustrated in the life of William Carey. He spent thirty-five years as a missionary to India, but you could count on your hand the people he won to Jesus Christ. After six months I would have said, "God, are You sure this is where I belong?" But every missionary who has ever gone to India since owes his missionary work to William Carey. He spent thirty-five years translating the Word of God into various dialects of India. Every other missionary effort that's been carried on there has been based on his work. I'm thankful to God that he knew something about the patience of faith.

B. The Passages

1. 2 Thessalonians 1:4—Paul says, "So that we ourselves glory in you in the churches of God for your patience and faith in all your persecutions and tribulations that ye endure." In other words, Paul was excited about the fact that they persevered when the going got tough.

2. Hebrews 12:1—"Wherefore, seeing we also are compassed about with so great a cloud of witnesses, let us lay aside every weight, and the sin which doth so easily beset us, and let us run with patience the race that is set before us."

3. James 1:3-4—"Knowing this, that the testing of your faith worketh patience. But let patience have her perfect work, that ye may be perfect and entire, lacking nothing."

4. James 5:7-8, 11—"Be patient therefore, brethren, unto the coming of the Lord. Behold, the farmer waiteth for the precious fruit of the earth, and hath long patience for it, until he receive the early and latter rain. Be ye also patient, establish your hearts; for the coming of the Lord draweth nigh. . . . Behold, we count them happy who endure. Ye have heard of the patience of Job, and have seen the end of the Lord, that the Lord is very pitiful and of tender mercy."

You may say, "I've been praying to the Lord for two weeks about a situation. When is He going to resolve it?" Be patient. I know people who have prayed for something for thirty years—even forty, fifty, or sixty years. Sometimes we run out of the patience of faith. We say, "Well, I guess God is never going to do that." Be patient. That's what made Abraham's life the complete life of faith. Faith is deaf to doubt, dumb to discouragement, blind to impossibilities, and, as a result, knows only success.

C. The Perspective

What was the secret of Abraham's patience? Hebrews 11:10 says, "For he looked for a city which hath foundations, whose builder and maker is God." Abraham wasn't looking down; he was looking up. He was patient because he was aware of the fact that heaven was waiting.

In the Greek text there is a definite article before the words *city* and *foundations.* It literally reads, "For he looked for the city which hath the foundations, whose builder and maker is God." Abraham was patient because he knew where he was going. That's the patience of faith.

1. Ezekiel 48:35b—"The name of the city from that day shall be, The Lord is there." If we keep our eyes on the fact that we're going to be in His presence in that city, then we can be patient with what is going on here.

2. Colossians 3:2—When we set our affections on things on this earth we live and die with everything that happens. That's why Paul said, "Set your affection on things above, not on things on the earth." When you do that, you will be patient with what happens on earth.

3. Genesis 13:12—Lot was a contrast to Abraham. Abraham didn't care about earthly luxuries. He lived in a tent, moving from place to place over Canaan. But Lot "dwelt in the cities of the plain, and pitched his tent toward Sodom." Lot wanted to have what the world offered. Lot wanted the earthly; Abraham wanted the heavenly. Abraham didn't care anything about the earth, but Lot did.

   If you continually look at the things of this world—trials, troubles, struggles, money, fame, entertainment, pleasure—then you become absorbed in the impatient desire of the flesh. But if you just focus on heaven and Jesus Christ, you won't care about what happens on earth.

4. 2 Timothy 2:3-4a—"Thou, therefore, endure hardness, as a good soldier of Jesus Christ." Why? "No man that warreth entangleth himself with the affairs of *this* life" (emphasis added). If you're fighting God's battle you're not going to get tangled up in the world.

5. Hebrews 11:27—"By faith he [Moses] forsook Egypt, not fearing the wrath of the king; for he endured." How

did Moses endure forty years in the wilderness tending sheep? Verse 27 says, "As seeing him [God] who is invisible." In Greek the word translated "as" can also mean "while." Moses endured while he was seeing Him who is invisible. He was able to stay forty years in the wilderness because he never took his eyes off God and was never disturbed with what was going on around him. He had his focus on the right place.

6. Hebrews 12:1b-2a—"Let us run with patience the race that is set before us, looking unto Jesus." We are to run the race looking at Jesus. Have you ever tried watching your feet while you were running a race? You'd probably run into things. You have to focus on a distant point. As a Christian you have to set your eyes on Jesus. Only when you do that will you see how close you are to the finish. If you run the race looking a few feet ahead, you'll never see any farther than that. And if you never see the finish line you'll never know you're getting there. But if you remember that every day is one day closer to Jesus Christ, then the race can be run with patience.

Hebrews 10:36 says, "For ye have need of patience that, after ye had done the will of God, ye might receive the promise." You may say, "I've been serving the Lord a long time, and I don't seem to be getting any benefits." Be patient—that's part of faith. People who live by faith are patient. Some people say, "Oh, what's God doing? My world is falling apart." They do not exhibit the patience of faith. Abraham waited until God did things in His own time. There's no reason for Christians to be anxious. Paul says in Philippians 4:6a, "Be anxious for nothing."

III. THE POWER OF FAITH (vv. 11-12)

Faith is powerful—it sees the invisible, hears the inaudible, touches the intangible, and accomplishes the impossible. "Through faith also Sarah herself received strength to conceive seed, and was delivered of a child when she was past age, because she judged him faithful who had promised." Faith brought a miracle. It was humanly impossible for Abraham and Sarah to have a baby. Sarah was ninety years old, and Abraham was ninety-nine. They were both past the age of conceiving a child.

Verse 12 says, "Therefore sprang there even of one, and him as good as dead, as many as the stars of the sky in multitude, and the sand which is by the seashore innumerable." Abraham had children upon children—the whole nation of Israel. Every Jew that's ever been born—or will ever be born—is of the seed of Abraham. Faith is powerful!

A. Matthew 19:26—"Jesus beheld them, and said unto them, With men this is impossible, but with God all things are possible."

B. Mark 9:23—"Jesus said unto him, If thou canst believe, all things are possible to him that believeth."

C. Luke 18:27—Jesus said, "The things which are impossible with men are possible with God." Do you believe God for the impossible?

D. Matthew 17:19-20—"Then came the disciples to Jesus privately, and said, Why could not we cast him [a demon, v. 16] out? And Jesus said unto them, Because of your unbelief; for verily I say unto you, If ye have faith as a grain of mustard seed [a thriving, increasing, growing faith], ye shall say unto this mountain, Move from here to yonder place; and it shall move; and nothing shall be impossible unto you."

E. Philippians 4:13—"I can do all things through Christ, who strengtheneth me."

F. Ephesians 3:20—"Now unto him who is able to do exceedingly abundantly above all that we ask or think, according to the power that worketh in us."

Are you believing God for the things that look like they require miracles to be accomplished? Do you believe God for those things? Nothing is too hard for God.

IV. THE POSITIVISM OF FAITH (vv. 13-16)

Abraham, Isaac, and Jacob never had the Promised Land in their possession. Yet verses 13-16 say, "These all died in faith, not having received the promises but having seen them afar off, and were persuaded [were positive] of them, and embraced them, and confessed that they were strangers and pilgrims on the earth. For they that say such things declare plainly that they seek a country [they were looking for another place]. And truly, if they had been mindful of that country from which they came out, they might have had opportunity to return [they weren't looking back to the country they came from, either]. But now they desire a better country, that is, an heavenly . . ." Those men were happy to be strangers and pilgrims on this earth because they knew there was a positive end to their faith.

Notice that they are called "strangers and pilgrims on the earth" in verse 13. The Greek word for "strangers" is *xenoi*. In the ancient world a stranger often faced a difficult fate. He was regarded with hatred, suspicion, and contempt. The word also came to mean "refugee." They were nomads in the worst sense of the word. They were also called "pilgrims," or *parepidemoi*. This referred to a person who stayed temporarily. They knew they were on shifting sand and that their mission in this world was limited. They sought for something greater and were sure about it—even though they never saw it.

A. Our Security

Are you sure about heaven? Are you *really* sure? The positivism of faith says, "I'm sure about heaven. I know it's there because I have witness of the Spirit of God within me, and I just long to be there."

1. Psalm 27:4a—David said, "One thing have I desired of the Lord, that I will seek after: that I may dwell in the house of the Lord all the days of my life." That is the positivism of faith—the security of the believer.

2. Job 19:26-27b—God allowed Satan to take away everything Job had—he was destitute. Finally he said, "Though after my skin worms destroy this body, yet in

my flesh shall I see God . . . though my heart be consumed within me." Job knew where he was going.

3. Philippians 1:23—Paul in essence said to the Philippians, "It's nice to be around you people; I like you a lot. But it's far better to go and be with Christ." That is our security.

B. Our Special Honor

Verse 16b says, "God is not ashamed to be called their God; for he hath prepared for them a city." God is not ashamed of those who believe Him and live by faith. In 1 Samuel 2:30b God says, "For them who honor me I will honor." That should make a difference in how we live.

The patriarchs honored God, and God said, "I'm not ashamed to be called their God." Do you know what God called Himself? In Exodus 3:6a He says, "I am the God of thy father, the God of Abraham, the God of Isaac, and the God of Jacob." I can't think of any greater honor than to live a life of faith and to have God assign Himself to me. That's the positivism of faith.

V. THE PROOF OF FAITH (vv. 17-19)

"By faith Abraham, when he was tested, offered up Isaac; and he that had received the promises offered up his only begotten son, of whom it was said, In Isaac shall thy seed be called; accounting that God was able to raise him up, even from the dead, from which also he received him in a figure."

This story is told in detail in Genesis 22:1-18. After a long time of waiting God finally gave Abraham a child. Then one day God said to Abraham, "I want you to take that son I gave you, go up to Mount Moriah, and offer him as a sacrifice." Abraham responded to God in obedience. He packed his gear, and along with Isaac and two other young men he set out toward Mount Moriah. Three days later when their destination was in sight, Abraham said to the two young men that were with him, "Abide ye here . . . I and the lad will go yonder and worship, and come again to you" (v. 5). Abraham knew that God told him to give Isaac as a sacrifice. But Abraham also knew

87

that the covenant of God was unconditional. He believed that God would raise Isaac from the dead. Hebrews 11:19 says, "Accounting that God was able to raise him up, even from the dead." What a tremendous act of faith!

That took monumental faith for many reasons: (1) all of Abraham's dreams were in Isaac; (2) there was a confusion between divine promise and divine command; (3) Abraham loved Isaac; (4) Abraham had waited a long time for the first sign of the promise; (5) Abraham may have thought that because of his sin with Hagar God was going to take away the promise; (6) God's law forbade a person to kill another (Gen. 9:6). All of those thoughts must have run through Abraham's mind—but he trusted God. He said, "God, if You want me to offer him as a sacrifice I will. But if I do, I know You'll raise him from the dead because You promised me that he would be the seed." That's faith. Do you have the faith to say, "God, I'll do whatever You say because I believe in Your promises"?

Abraham bound Isaac, laid him on the altar, and raised the knife to slay him. But the angel of the Lord called out to him to stop him and provided a ram for the sacrifice instead. Isaac became a picture of the death and resurrection of Christ—"from which also he received him in a figure" (v. 19b).

What is the final proof of faith? Sacrificial obedience. Jesus said, "If any man will come after me, let him deny himself, and take up his cross, and follow me" (Matt. 16:24).

Focusing on the Facts

1. What makes Abraham a good model of the life of faith (see p. 74)?
2. In what three ways was Abraham's faith manifested (Heb. 11:8; see p. 75)?
3. True or false: Abraham was raised in a godly environment (see pp. 75-76).
4. Salvation demands _____ (see p. 76).
5. Define worldliness (see p. 78).
6. What is one way to measure your level of spiritual maturity (see p. 79)?
7. In what way was Abraham's patience manifested (see p. 80)?

8. True or false: After years of patient waiting Abraham saw God's promise fulfilled (see p. 81).
9. What motivated Abraham to be patient in his faith (see pp. 82-83)?
10. What are some of the reasons God's command to sacrifice Isaac was such a severe test of Abraham's faith (see p. 88)?

Pondering the Principles

1. Hebrews 11:8 implies that Abraham's obedience to God's call was immediate. We are sometimes tempted not to obey God right away. However, delayed obedience is disobedience. Do you sense Him directing you to do something but find yourself procrastinating? Do you have an opportunity to serve in a ministry or meet a need that you are hesitating to become involved with? Or is the Holy Spirit convicting you to forsake some sin? Follow the example of Abraham, and obey God immeadiately.

2. Just as Abraham was a stranger and pilgrim in the Promised Land, so Christians are strangers in this world. Our citizenship is in heaven (Phil. 3:20), and our earthly existence is temporary. Do your priorities reflect that fact, or are you in danger of becoming so earthly minded that you're no heavenly good? Are your goals in life different from those of your non-Christian friends, or are you pursuing the same things they are? Meditate on our Lord's words in Matthew 6:33 this week, and ask God to show you where your priorities do not match up with His program.

6
Faith in the Face of Death

Outline

Introduction
A. Their Covenant
B. Their Confidence

Lesson
I. Isaac (v. 20)
  A. His Failures (Gen. 26:2-25)
    1. Disobedience (vv. 2-6)
    2. Lying (vv. 7-11)
    3. Cowardice (vv. 7-11)
    4. Resignation (vv. 15-22)
  B. His Family (Gen. 25:21-34)
    1. The appeal of Isaac (v. 21)
    2. The prophecy of the Lord (vv. 22-23)
    3. The birth of the twins (vv. 24-26)
    4. The preference of the parents (vv. 27-28)
    5. The procurement of the birthright (vv. 29-34)
  C. His Faith (Gen. 27:1-33)
    1. Isaac's plan (vv. 1-4)
    2. Rebekah's plot (vv. 5-17)
    3. Jacob's performance (vv. 18-29)
    4. Isaac's pronouncement (vv. 30-33)
II. Jacob (v. 21)
III. Joseph (v. 22)

Introduction

Commentator Matthew Henry said, "Though the grace of faith is of universal use throughout our whole lives, yet it is especially so when we come to die. Faith has its great work to do at last, to help believers to finish well, to die to the Lord, so as to honour him, by patience, hope and joy—so as to leave a witness behind them of the truth of God's word and the excellency of his ways" (*Commentary on the Whole Bible*, vol. 6 [New York: Revell, n.d.], p. 946). God is greatly glorified when His people leave this world with their flag flying at full mast. If anyone should die triumphantly it should be the believer. When the Spirit triumphs over the flesh, when the world is consciously and gladly left behind for heaven, when there's anticipation in the soul and glory in the eyes as we enter into the presence of the Lord—then we're dying as pleasing unto the Lord.

In Hebrews 11:20-22 the Holy Spirit presents three great examples of men who, when they faced death, were full of faith. "By faith Isaac blessed Jacob and Esau concerning things to come. By faith Jacob, when he was dying, blessed both the sons of Joseph, and worshiped, leaning upon the top of his staff. By faith Joseph, when he died, made mention of the departing of the children of Israel, and gave commandment concerning his bones."

As you read that passage you may have thought, *How is he going to get anything out of that?* There is actually much material behind these verses, and the writer of Hebrews expected the Jewish readers to fill in the history themselves. They understood the background. Unfortunately we can't do that as readily, so we'll spend more time considering this.

A. Their Covenant

The point that the writer of Hebrews wants to get across is that these men died without ever having seen the fulfillment of God's promise. But before they died they passed it on to their children by faith. God appeared to Abraham and made a covenant with Him. Basically, the Abrahamic covenant promised three things:

1. The possession of the land

2. A great nation

3. Spiritual blessing to the world

B. Their Confidence

Neither Abraham, Isaac, Jacob, nor Joseph saw any of these things come to pass. Yet they were so confident in the promises of God that they passed them on to their children. Hebrews 11:13 says, "These [Abraham, Isaac, and Jacob] all died in faith, not having received the promises but having seen them afar off, and were persuaded of them, and embraced them, and confessed that they were strangers and pilgrims on the earth." They had not seen the fulfillment, yet they believed that their children would see fulfillment. Why? Because God always keeps His Word. They believed it even though they never saw it. They didn't die in the despair of unfulfilled dreams, saying, "It never came." They died saying, "It will come." They believed God. They died defeating death because they knew the promise of God would never die.

They had magnificent faith. If we could have read their minds and listened to their thoughts, perhaps we would have heard them say, "God's promise of a people and the possession of this land must be true, for God never breaks a promise. I may not live to see it, but I know it will come. I may just be a link in the chain of fulfillment." It's important, then, to establish these men as men of faith, because they faced death with true faith.

Lesson

I. ISAAC (v. 20)

"By faith Isaac blessed Jacob and Esau concerning things to come."

93

The writer of Hebrews says little about Isaac in verse 20. The reader would have been familiar with him. It is interesting, however, that even though Isaac lived longer than the other three patriarchs mentioned, he has the least written about him in the book of Genesis. The other patriarchs have around twelve chapters each devoted to them, but Isaac's story is condensed into two chapters (Gen. 26-27) with a few other references. Perhaps the reason for this was that Isaac was the least spectacular. He was ordinary—rather passive, relatively quiet, and spiritually weak. He was the unspectacular son of a spectacular father and the unspectacular father of a spectacular son. There wasn't too much to say about him.

A. His Failures (Gen. 26:2-25)

1. Disobedience (vv. 2-6)

God told Isaac to sojourn in the land that he was presently in, the land of Gerar, and dwell only where He told him to dwell. But verse 6 shows Isaac's disobedience: "Isaac *dwelt* in Gerar" (emphasis added).

2. Lying (vv. 7-11)

Isaac lied to the men of Gerar and told them that Rebekah was not his wife but his sister.

3. Cowardice (vv. 7-11)

Isaac was a coward. The reason he lied and said that Rebekah was his sister is found in verses 7 and 9. He had a beautiful wife. He thought, *If I say this is my wife they'll kill me to get her.* He didn't seem concerned about whether they took her or not—he cared about staying alive.

Verses 12-14 show the unconditional nature of the Abrahamic covenant. Even though Isaac was a poor example from time to time, God still blessed and protected him.

4. Resignation (vv. 15-22)

The Philistines wanted to get Isaac out of their land, so they filled up his wells with dirt, cutting off his water supply. But Isaac would not leave the land completely.

He kept moving to a new spot and digging another well. Each time he dug another well, the Philistines filled it. Isaac didn't put up any resistance—he passively went somewhere else and started digging another well.

Finally in verse 23 Isaac sneaks in the back door of the Promised Land. The only way God could get him there was to have the Philistines keep filling up his wells. It took a lot to get him home; but he finally arrived. In a sense he was like the prodigal son, because when he arrived God threw His arms around him and blessed him (v. 24). That's how grace operates.

Isaac's life was weak and sinful, yet he believed God and established himself in the scroll of faith. How? By one great act that wrapped up his life. It's interesting, though, that he backed into that one, too. He finally wound up doing the right thing only because everybody set it up so he couldn't help but do the right thing. We'll look at that a little later.

B. His Family (Gen. 25:21-34)

1. The appeal of Isaac (v. 21)

Isaac faced the same problem that his father Abraham faced—his wife was barren. So Isaac entreated the Lord on behalf of Rebekah.

2. The prophecy of the Lord (vv. 22-23)

The Lord answered Isaac's prayer, and Rebekah conceived twins. In verse 23 the Lord tells Rebekah that the older of the two children would serve the younger. Now this was contrary to the law of primogeniture, which stated that the eldest son received the right of inheritance as well as the leadership of the family. But God reversed this and promised, even before they were born, that the elder would serve the younger.

3. The birth of the twins (vv. 24-26)

"The first came out red, all over like an hairy garment; and they called his name Esau. And after that came his brother out, and his hand took hold on Esau's heel; and his name was called Jacob." Even though Esau had the right of the firstborn, God sovereignly designed that Jacob would rule over Esau and be in the line of the Messiah. The fact that Jacob took hold of Esau's heel was symbolic of the fact that he would grasp Esau's birthright.

The Sovereignty of God

In Romans 9:11-13 Paul says that God chose Jacob over Esau on the basis of His absolute sovereignty. He said, "For the children being not yet born, neither having done any good or evil, that the purpose of God according to election might stand, not of works, but of him that calleth, it was said unto her, The elder shall serve the younger. As it is written, Jacob have I loved, but Esau have I hated." In other words God said, "I have the right to choose whomever I will. I choose Jacob." He made this choice before they were ever born or ever did right or wrong.

Paul expected his readers to respond, "That's not fair!" so in verses 14-15 he says, "What shall we say then? Is there unrighteousness with God? God forbid. For he saith to Moses, I will have mercy on whom I will have mercy, and I will have compassion on whom I will have compassion." God does what He wants.

Someone may say, "He can't do that. It's not right!" Paul answers that objection in verses 20-21: "Nay but, O man, who art thou that repliest against God? Shall the thing formed say to him that formed it, Why hast thou made me thus? Hath not the potter power over the clay, of the same lump to make one vessel unto honor, and another unto dishonor?" The potter has the right to make any kind of vessel he wants. Don't question the sovereignty of God.

Before the world was created, no man had a right to tell God to create it or not to create it—no man existed, and God did what He wanted. That which was left inert in creation had no reason to complain that it wasn't vegetative in nature. Nor did vegetables have any reason to complain that they weren't animals. Nor did animals have any reason to complain that they weren't men. Nor did our first parents have any reason to complain that they were created inferior to angels (cf. Heb. 2:7). Nothing had any claim to make on its Maker. If man had no claim on God when he was innocent, did he gain some claim after the Fall? Not at all.

In the human realm I reserve the right to bestow favor upon whomever I choose. Am I going to claim something for myself that God doesn't have? As we are objects of His grace, we have no one to thank but God. God is God, and He does what His sovereignty designs to do.

4. The preference of the parents (vv. 27-28)

"The boys grew: and Esau was a skillful hunter, a man of the field; and Jacob was a quiet man, dwelling in tents. And Isaac loved Esau." Why? "Because he did eat of his venison." Isaac attached himself to Esau because he was a materialistic, fleshly, lustful man who liked good meat. He craved meat, and Esau provided it. "But Rebekah loved Jacob." Why? Because he was a homebody, a cook in his mother's kitchen.

5. The procurement of the birthright (vv. 29-34)

Esau sold his birthright to Jacob for a bowl of lentil stew and a piece of bread. He was hungry, and he wanted something in his stomach. In fact, he was a lot like his father—if his stomach was full he was happy. Esau didn't care about the future; he was a pragmatist. He sold his birthright to Jacob. Verse 34 says, "Then Jacob gave Esau bread and pottage of lentils; and he did eat and drink, and rose up, and went his way: thus Esau despised his birthright." He had no thought for God. He was passionate, impulsive, and incapable of estimating the true value of anything that didn't immediately appeal to his senses—preferring the physical to the spiritual. He was profane (cf. Heb. 12:16).

C. His Faith (Gen. 27:1-33)

In Genesis 27 a drama takes place that ends with Isaac's ultimate act of faith. In fact, this is the act of faith referred to in Hebrews 11:20.

97

1. Isaac's plan (vv. 1-4)

   Isaac wanted Esau to receive the birthright in spite of
   the fact that God had told Rebekah it would go to Jacob
   and in spite of the fact that Esau had already sold it to Jacob. In verses 1-4 Isaac tries to sneak the blessing on
   Esau and circumvent prophecy. When he did that, he
   started a chain reaction of evil events that was Satan's
   effort to thwart God's plan. God twisted them around,
   however, and brought His plan to pass.

2. Rebekah's plot (vv. 5-17)

   Rebekah overheard Isaac talking to Esau, and she immediately sprang into action. She was a deceitful, proud,
   selfish woman who wanted her own way, not the
   Lord's. She showed a lack of faith in God because God
   could have brought about His plan in His own way. But
   she believed that she had to give God help—just like
   Sarah when she used Hagar to give Abraham a child.

   Rebekah plotted with Jacob to beat Esau out of his blessing. First, she decided that she would make Isaac's fa-
   vorite dish for Jacob to give to him. Jacob said that even
   though Isaac was blind, if he touched his skin he would
   know that it wasn't Esau who served him, because Esau
   was hairy and Jacob was smooth. To make sure Jacob
   wasn't discovered, Rebekah not only put the hairy skin
   of a baby goat on Jacob's hands and neck so that he
   would feel like Esau, but she also put Esau's best clothes
   on him so that he had Esau's scent.

3. Jacob's performance (vv. 18-29)

   Jacob's award-winning performance is recorded in
   verses 18-29. With his lying and deceit he ended up with
   the blessing of Isaac.

4. Isaac's pronouncement (vv. 30-33)

   Jacob had left when Esau walked in. When Isaac realized he'd been tricked, he "trembled very exceedingly,
   and said, Who? Where is he that hath taken venison,

and brought it me, and I have eaten of all before thou camest, and have blessed him? Yea, and he shall be blessed" (v. 33).

I believe Isaac paused a long time before saying, "Yea, and he shall be blessed." This is the one great faithful act in the life of Isaac. He realized that against his own will, against his own plot, and against his own fleshly design for Esau—God had granted the blessing to Jacob. So he said, "All right, God, he shall remain blessed. If that's what You insist upon, I'll accept it."

Keep in mind that whether Isaac blessed Jacob or Esau, he did believe in the Abrahamic promise being passed to one of his two sons. His faith was legitimate. He finally became obedient, even though it was against his will. When God wants to work His purposes He'll work them.

Isaac faced death with the absolute confidence that God would carry on after he was gone and fulfill His promise in his children.

II. JACOB (v. 21)

"By faith Jacob, when he was dying, blessed both the sons of Joseph, and worshiped, leaning upon the top of his staff."

The life of faith for Jacob was like that of his father, Isaac. It wasn't the shining of the sun on a clear day, its rays meeting with no resistance from the atmosphere; rather it was more like the sun rising on a foggy day, its rays struggling to pierce through the mist. Jacob was an up-and-down individual. Sometimes he walked by faith while other times he walked by sight. In spite of all his faults and failings, Jacob highly prized his interest in the everlasting One: He was anxious for the Lord to be his God (Gen. 28:21); he glorified God when making a covenant with Laban (Gen. 31:53); and although he was afraid of Esau he sought the Lord (Gen. 32:9-12). He was a man of faith, even though his faith didn't maintain itself throughout his whole life. But during the closing time of his life he believed the promise of God enough to pass it on to Joseph's two sons, Ephraim and Manasseh.

Genesis 48 records the blessing that Jacob gave Ephraim and Manasseh: "It came to pass after these things, that one told Joseph, Behold, thy father is sick: and he took with him his two sons, Manasseh and Ephraim. And one told Jacob, and said, Behold, thy son, Joseph, cometh unto thee; and Israel [Jacob] strengthened himself, and sat upon the bed" (vv. 1-2). Hebrews said that he leaned upon his staff. Put the two together and you find that he sat on the edge of the bed and leaned on his staff. That's what it's saying. He was weak and in bed, but he sat up and got his staff to support himself so that he could bless Joseph's sons with the promise of God.

"Jacob said unto Joseph, God Almighty appeared unto me at Luz [Bethel] in the land of Canaan, and blessed me, and said unto me, Behold, I will make thee fruitful, and multiply thee, and I will make of thee a multitude of people; and will give this land to thy seed after thee for an everlasting possession" (vv. 3-4). Even though Jacob never saw any of this, he still believed God. He believed that God would fulfill His promise—if not to him, then to his heirs. So he passed on the promise to the sons of Joseph.

"Now thy two sons, Ephraim and Manasseh, who were born unto thee in the land of Egypt before I came unto thee into Egypt, are mine; as Reuben and Simeon, they shall be mine" (v. 5). In other words, "Just as if they were firstborn, they shall be mine." How did Jacob know to bless these two? God revealed it to him, and he obeyed. He believed that God's promise would be fulfilled in these two young men.

"Israel [Jacob] beheld Joseph's sons, and said, Who are these? And Joseph said unto his father, They are my sons, whom God hath given me in this place" (vv. 8-9). Jacob said, "Bring them, I pray thee, unto me, and I will bless them. Now the eyes of Israel [Jacob] were dim for age, so that he could not see. And he brought them near unto him; and he kissed them, and embraced them. And Israel said unto Joseph, I had not thought to see thy face; and, lo, God hath shown me also thy seed. And Joseph brought them out from between his knees, and he bowed himself with his face to the earth. And Joseph took them both, Ephraim in his right hand toward Israel's left hand, and Manasseh in his left toward Israel's right hand, and brought them near unto him" (vv. 9-13). The blessing was done with the right hand, so Joseph placed Manasseh, the firstborn, at his left side, but Jacob placed his right hand on the head of Ephraim, who was the younger, and his left hand upon Manasseh's head, "guiding his hands knowingly; for Manasseh was the first-born."

Verses 15-16 say, "He blessed Joseph, and said, God, before whom my fathers, Abraham and Isaac, did walk, the God who fed me all my life long unto this day, an angel who redeemed me from all evil, bless the lads; and let my name be named on them, and the name of my fathers, Abraham and Isaac; and let them grow into a multitude in the midst of the earth."

"When Joseph saw that his father laid his right hand upon the head of Ephraim, it displeased him; and he held up his father's hand, to remove it from Ephraim's head unto Manasseh's head" (v. 17). Even though Manasseh was the firstborn, here again was a turning away from the firstborn as God was working His plan. "Joseph said unto his father, Not so, my father; for this is the first-born; put thy right hand upon his head. And his father refused, and said, I know it, my son, I know it" (vv. 18-19). If he knew that, why did he bless Ephraim? Because he was following the command of God. "He also shall become a people, and he also shall be great; but truly his younger brother shall be greater than he, and his seed shall become a multitude of nations. And he blessed them that day, saying, In thee shall Israel bless, saying, God make thee as Ephraim and Manasseh: and he set Ephraim before Manasseh. And Israel said unto Joseph, Behold I die; but God shall be with you, and bring you again unto the land of your fathers" (vv. 19-21).

Jacob believed that God would fulfill His promise completely. Jacob died as a man of faith just as his father, Isaac, had died.

III. JOSEPH (v. 22)

"By faith Joseph, when he died, made mention of the departing of the children of Israel, and gave commandment concerning his bones."

Joseph was dying, and he knew that his body would have to be buried in Egypt, where he spent the greater portion of his life. It had been more than two hundred years since the promise had been given to Abraham as recorded in Genesis 15:13-16, and it still hadn't been fulfilled. But Joseph believed God's promise—his faith was strong. Genesis 50:24-26 says, "Joseph said unto his brethren, I die; and God will surely visit you, and bring you out of this land unto the land which He swore to give to Abraham, to Isaac, and to Jacob. And Joseph took an oath of the children of Israel, saying, God will surely visit you, and ye shall carry up my bones from here. So Joseph died, being an hundred and ten years old: and they embalmed him, and he was put in a coffin in Egypt." He was buried in Egypt, dying in faith.

Did they ever get his bones out of Egypt? Yes. Exodus 13:19 says, "Moses took the bones of Joseph with him; for he had solemnly sworn the children of Israel, saying, God will surely visit you, and ye shall carry up my bones away from here with you." When they left they took Joseph's remains with them.

The three men we looked at all believed God in the face of death. All their dreams were unrealized, yet they died victoriously. That is the acid test of a man's faith. How does it hold up in the face of death? If his faith doesn't hold up, it's no good.

Two Reasons That People Fear Death

1. For themselves—The first reason that people fear death is because they're afraid of what will happen to them. If you're a Christian, there's nothing to fear, because when you die you'll be in the presence of the Lord (2 Cor. 5:8). A Christian should not fear death. First Corinthians 15:55 says, "O death, where is thy sting? O grave, where is thy victory?" Jesus has conquered death. Do you believe that Jesus has prepared a place for you in the Father's house? If so, you have nothing to fear.

2. For others—Some people ask, "If I die, who is going to carry on the work?" That's ridiculous. God has a perfect plan, and His work will go on.

Let me say this, however, to you who may not know God: you had better fear death. Death will separate you from God and all that is good.

Focusing on the Facts

1. What do Isaac, Jacob, and Joseph all have in common concerning their faith (see p. 92)?
2. Name the three basic features of the Abrahamic covenant (see pp. 92-93).
3. True or false: Although Isaac lived longer than either Abraham, Jacob, or Joseph, the book of Genesis devotes less space to his life than to theirs (see pp. 93-94).
4. Why was it wrong for Isaac to live in the land of Gerar (see p. 94)?
5. How did God finally get Isaac into the Promised Land (see p. 95)?
6. Why was it unusual for the older of Isaac's sons to serve the younger (see p. 95)?
7. True or false: God chose Jacob over Esau because of Esau's sinful life (see p. 96).
8. In what way was Esau like his father (see p. 97)?
9. Describe how God brought about His plan despite the scheming of Isaac, Rebekah, and Jacob (see pp. 97-99).
10. How was Isaac's faith ultimately manifested (see p. 99)?
11. How would you characterize Jacob's faith throughout his life (see p. 99)?
12. How was Jacob's faith ultimately manifested (see p. 99)?
13. How was Joseph's faith ultimately manifested (see p. 101)?
14. Give two reasons why people fear death. Are they legitimate? Explain your answer (see p. 102).

Pondering the Principles

1. Isaac, Jacob, and Joseph all passed on to their children God's promises of blessing. What legacy are you passing on? Are you passing on a legacy of holy living and faith in God, or one of worldliness and sin? If you have children, do they see your faith reflected in your daily life? Do you spend time systematically instructing them in the truths of God's Word? If you do not have a time of family devotions, now is the time to begin. See your pastor or youth pastor if you need some ideas on how to structure that time. Most important of all, let your children see the principles of God's Word lived out in your life. The greatest inheri-

tance we can leave our children is not material wealth but a living faith in God.

2. God's sovereignty was manifested in his choice of Jacob over Esau. God is no less sovereign over the circumstances of your life. Spend some time this week thinking back over the events of your life. Praise God for the times He helped you through a difficult experience or blessed you. Then thank Him for all the difficult things He allowed you to go through, remembering that all trials in a believer's life are for a purpose (James 1:2-4). Events that seem good to us and those we don't like both fall under God's sovereignty. Finally, thank God for sovereignly choosing you to be saved.

7
Things Faith Accepts and Rejects—Part 1

Outline

Introduction
A. The Everyday Opportunity of Making Right Decisions
B. The Exhortations to Make the Right Decision
  1. Deuteronomy 30:19
  2. Joshua 24:15
  3. 1 Kings 18:21
C. The Examples of Some Who Made the Right Decision
  1. Hebrews 11
    a) Abel
    b) Enoch
    c) Noah
    d) Abraham
    e) Isaac, Jacob, and Joseph
  2. 1 Kings 19:18
  3. Nehemiah 10:28-29
  4. 2 Kings 22:2
D. The Enemy of Making Right Decisions

Lesson
I. Things Faith Rejects (vv. 24-27)
  A. The World's Prestige (v. 24)
    1. Moses' preparation
      a) In the wisdom of messianic hope
      b) In the wisdom of Egypt
    2. Moses' decision
      a) His call
      b) His choice
        (1) Responding to God's call
        (2) Refusing the honor of the palace

B. The World's Pleasures (v. 25)
  1. Job 20:5
  2. Job 21:7-13
  3. Psalm 73:12-19
  4. Isaiah 21:4*b*
  5. James 5:5

Introduction

The book of Hebrews was written to Jewish readers. In chapter 11 the writer wants his Jewish readers to understand the absolute priority of faith. That is important, because in Judaism at this particular time works had become the dominant factor. So the point he is making is that the New Covenant (chaps. 1-10) is only received by faith, not works. God is not approached by works, religiosity, ceremony, or ritual. He is only approached by simple faith—believing in Him and trusting in Him apart from any personal works. That's his point, and it is repeated over and over again.

Faith was a foreign commodity to the readers of the book of Hebrews. They were so used to works as a way to God that they needed to be given a step-by-step understanding of faith. And so they wouldn't think that faith was some kind of heresy, the writer of Hebrews used all Old Testament people as illustrations. That's nothing new; God has always operated on the basis of faith apart from a religious system.

The Old Testament saints have shown us a great deal about faith already: Abel showed us how to live by faith (pp. 24-35); Enoch showed us how to walk by faith (pp. 40-54); Abraham showed us the pattern of faith (pp. 73-88); Isaac, Jacob, and Joseph showed us the victory of faith in the face of death (pp. 92-102); and now we will consider Moses, who will show us how to make decisions or choices of faith.

Moses was a man of great faith. Even before the system of commandments that he received on Mount Sinai he believed God. That was the key to his life. He set a great standard for us in the decisions that true faith must make.

A. The Everyday Opportunity of Making Right Decisions

Life is made up of decisions. When you wake up in the morning you decide whether or not you will get out of bed. You decide what to wear. You decide what to eat for breakfast. You go through life in a continual process of making decisions.

One aspect of Christian maturity is the ability to make right decisions. A mature Christian will consistently make right decisions, while an immature Christian will not. In other words, holiness is making right decisions; carnality is making wrong ones. In terms of maturity and holiness your Christian life rises or falls on the basis of the decisions that you make. For example:

1. When Satan tempts you decide either to say no or yes.

2. When a witnessing opportunity arises you either take the time to communicate the truth of Jesus Christ or you don't.

3. When you have spare time you either study the Bible or you don't.

4. When you wake up Sunday morning you either go to church and have fellowship or you don't.

Invariably the decisions that we make touch every area of our Christian lives. Since the beginning of time God has given us the opportunity to make choices that will affect our lives. The first people that had a choice to make were Adam and Eve. Unfortunately they made the wrong one. Every turn of life hinges on the decisions that we make—we either grasp every opportunity for the glory of God or we miss opportunities by choosing the way of the flesh, the world, and Satan.

B. The Exhortations to Make the Right Decision

The way people decide will determine their destiny—both temporal and eternal. God calls all people to make a choice.

1. Deuteronomy 30:19—"I call heaven and earth to record this day against you, that I have set before you life and death, blessing and cursing; therefore, choose life, that both thou and thy seed may live."

2. Joshua 24:15—"If it seem evil unto you to serve the Lord, choose you this day whom ye will serve . . . but as for me and my house, we will serve the Lord."

3. 1 Kings 18:21—"Elijah came unto all the people, and said, How long halt ye between two opinions? If the Lord be God, follow him; but if Baal, then follow him. And the people answered him not a word."

C. The Examples of Some Who Made the Right Decision

1. Hebrews 11

   a) Abel—Abel chose God's way—a more excellent sacrifice. His brother did not. Abel was blessed; his brother was cursed.

   b) Enoch—Enoch chose God's way and walked with Him. The rest of the world did not.

   c) Noah—Noah chose God's way, obeying Him and doing what He said. The rest of the world did not, and they drowned.

   d) Abraham—Abraham chose God's way, living a life of faith. The people in whose land he dwelt did not, and they were destroyed.

   e) Isaac, Jacob, and Joseph—They chose God's way, believed Him for what they couldn't see, and conquered death. The heathen refused to believe, and death conquered them.

2. 1 Kings 19:18—God said to Elijah, "Yet I have left me seven thousand in Israel, all the knees which have not bowed unto Baal, and every mouth which hath not kissed him."

3. Nehemiah 10:28-29—Here we see a long list of the people of Israel who took an oath and swore "to walk in God's law, which was given by Moses, the servant of God, and to observe and do all the commandments of the Lord . . . and his ordinances and his statutes." They made a right choice.

4. 2 Kings 22:2—King Josiah "did that which was right in the sight of the Lord . . . and turned not aside to the right hand or to the left."

D. The Enemy of Making Right Decisions

Right choices are made on the basis of faith, because sometimes the things that Satan throws in front of us are alluring to the flesh, and we don't see any immediate spiritual substitute as interesting. For example, Satan may come along and say, "If you do this in your business you'll probably make fifty thousand dollars. It might be a little shady, but go ahead and do it." And one may respond, "No, that would be wrong. I'd better do what the Lord wants. If I don't I will miss joy in my life. Let's see—joy or fifty thousand dollars? Well, I don't know . . ." And so it goes. Sometimes as we think about it the spiritual commodity that becomes ours isn't nearly as enticing. We have to say by faith, "God, I'm going to believe You although at this point I am tempted to pursue the money. I'm going to believe You and do what's right." That's how faith operates. Once you've done that, you've put up the shield of faith (Eph. 6:16).

Do you know what the shield of faith is? It is believing God. Every time you believe God, Satan's arrows are thwarted. When Satan comes along and says, "Do this," but you say, "I don't want to do that; God says to do this," the shield of faith is raised, and Satan's fiery darts are quenched. Just remember that every time you sin, you believed Satan rather than God. So if you don't want to sin start believing God. The shield against sin is faith.

The record of the life of Moses covers four of the five books of the Pentateuch—from Exodus 2 to Deuteronomy 34. Moses was a tremendous man, the greatest of the Old Testament figures. And his greatness was not based on legalism; it was based on his faith in God. He believed God in the midst of unbelievable circumstances.

Looking at the decisions he made gives us a great standard to follow.

Lesson

I. THINGS FAITH REJECTS (vv. 24-27)

A. The World's Prestige (v. 24)

"By faith Moses, when he was come to years [age forty; cf. Acts 7:23], refused to be called the son of Pharaoh's daughter."

Moses had risen to the heights of Egyptian society from a Hebrew baby that was supposed to have been killed by Pharaoh. The story is recorded for us in Exodus 1:22–2:10. Pharaoh had sent out an edict to have all of the newborn sons in Israel killed—thrown into the river. But the parents of Moses, Amram and Jochebed, hid him for three months. Once they couldn't hide him any longer, they put him in a basket in the river. When Pharaoh's daughter saw the basket, she opened it up, discovered baby Moses, and took him as her own son.

Moses grew up in the society of Egypt, the wealthiest, most advanced civilization in that part of the world. As the son of Pharaoh's daughter he was a prince and may have had the right to rule someday.

1. Moses' preparation

a) In the wisdom of messianic hope

Exodus 2:9 says, "Pharaoh's daughter said unto her [Moses' mother, Jochebed], Take this child away,

110

and nurse it for me. . . . And the woman took the child, and nursed him." Jochebed took Moses and weaned him. According to scholars this refers to a period of time lasting anywhere from three to twelve years. I believe Moses was in his parents' home somewhere close to twelve years, or at least long enough for them to have taught him the messianic hope. He stayed long enough to learn the promise of Abraham that had been reiterated to Isaac, Jacob, and Joseph. He stayed long enough to know that God had promised that His people would not only leave Egypt but also that He would give them a great deliverer. And, finally, he stayed long enough to learn of the Abrahamic covenant of a great nation, worldwide blessing, and possession of a land. All of that was, undoubtedly, taught to Moses.

b) In the wisdom of Egypt

After the training period with his parents was over, Moses rejoined the royal court as a prince of Egypt. He was in the position to receive everything Egypt had to offer. Stephen says in his sermon in Acts 7:22*a*, "Moses was learned in all the wisdom of the Egyptians." He had a fantastic education during those years. He was educated at the highest level, being educated in the house of Pharaoh and learning the things that only those in Pharaoh's house could teach. He was exposed to all the wisdom of the Egyptians.

Formal education in ancient Egypt included the reading and writing of hieroglyphic and hieratic scripts, the copying of texts, and learning all the languages of Canaan. I'm sure God used this education to refine his God-given ability to be a leader and to enable him to write the first five books of the Old Testament, the Pentateuch. All of this education went together to make him God's man. For forty years in Egypt God trained him and made him something. Then God used forty years in the desert to break him. And then for forty years He used him.

111

2. Moses' decision

a) His call

When Moses reached forty, he faced a crucial decision. He had to choose whether to become a full-fledged Egyptian or to join his own people, the people of Israel. He had a key to making the decision —his faith in God. All through those forty years he apparently never wavered in his faith in God. For forty years he had enjoyed the privileges, the prestige, the status, and the honors of a prince in Egypt. But when the time came to face the biggest decision of his life, it's apparent that God indicated to him that He wanted him to go back to his people and lead them out of Egypt to the Promised Land. Moses had to make a choice whether to throw aside everything that he had in the palace and go live with slaves or to forget the call of God and hold onto what he had.

b) His choice

(1) Responding to God's call

Stephen's sermon in Acts 7:23-25 reads, "When he was full forty years old, it came into his heart to visit his brethren, the children of Israel. And seeing one of them suffer wrong, he defended him, and avenged him that was oppressed, and smote the Egyptian. For he supposed his brethren would have understood how that God by his hand would deliver them; but they understood not."

Moses knew that God had already called him to be the deliverer, so he thought, *If I go in there and kill that Egyptian, it will prove to the people whose side I'm on. Then they'll know that I'm to be their deliverer.* They didn't accept him, but Moses knew what God wanted out of him, and he responded positively.

(2) Refusing the honor of the palace

> Hebrews 11 tells us that Moses forsook the honor of the palace. Verse 24 says, "By faith Moses, when he was come to years, refused to be called the son of Pharaoh's daughter." Moses did not seek the world's prestige; he sought the will of God. He knew God had a better kingdom and a better reward. Most people live their entire lives dreaming about attaining prestige, honor, and fame, but Moses gave them all up.

Evaluating Greatness: The World's Standards Versus God's Standards

The world has its own evaluation system. How do you get honor in this world? Usually in one of four ways:

1. Family—If you're born into the right family, you're honored and automatically thrust into the public eye with a measure of greatness, even though you may not have any.

2. Money—The world also uses money to measure prestige and honor. If you have a lot of wealth you'll be honored in the world. It may not be honest honor, but you'll receive it nevertheless.

3. Education—Many people believe that having degrees after your name is a characteristic of greatness and makes one worthy of honor.

4. Position—The last reason the world bestows honor and measures greatness is if you're famous for what you do—whether it's athletics, entertainment, finance, business, and so on.

But none of these things have any relation to God's standards for greatness. He honors people on a totally different basis. He's not interested in what family you came from, how much money you have, how much education you've had, or what position you have in the world. He's not even remotely concerned with any of these things in terms of greatness. Let me prove it to you by introducing you to a man who was greater than Moses, David, Abraham, Elijah, or any other Old Testament saint.

113

The greatest man who ever lived up until his time was John the Baptist. He wasn't considered great because of his family—he was born to a simple priest. He wasn't considered great because of his money—he lived in the desert and wore clothing made of camel's skin. He wasn't considered great because of his education—he had none. He wasn't considered great because of his position—he lived in the wilderness and ate locusts and wild honey. He had a simple family, no money, no education, and was a desert wanderer—yet Jesus tells us in Matthew 11:11a, "Among them that are born of women there hath not risen a greater than John the Baptist." What made him so great? Three things stand out (Luke 1:15-16):

1. He was obedient.

2. He was Spirit-filled.

3. He turned many of the hearts of the people of Israel to God.

God's measure of greatness is different from that of the world. What is to be our attitude towards the things of the world? John says in 1 John 2:15-17, "Love not the world, neither the things that are in the world. If any man love the world, the love of the Father is not in him. For all that is in the world, the lust of the flesh, and the lust of the eyes, and the pride of life, is not of the Father, but is of the world. And the world passeth away, and the lust of it; but he that doeth the will of God abideth forever."

Moses didn't care about all the things that the world had to offer. The world doesn't have much to offer when you compare it with what the Lord offers. Moses didn't choose the world's prestige. He chose, rather, to join the slaves of Israel and be their leader.

B. The World's Pleasures (v. 25)

"Choosing rather to suffer affliction with the people of God than to enjoy the pleasures of sin for a season."

Sin has enjoyable characteristics—for a season. Moses was called to give his life for his people, and he knew it. So he had a choice, a decision either to do what God told him to do or to disobey. It would have been pleasurable to disobey from a human standpoint. Moses could have lived in the palace, had all the goodies he wanted, had all the women he wanted, had all the money he wanted, had all the power he wanted, and had all the authority he wanted. But God told him to go to the Israelite slaves and assign himself to them. That's the choice he had to make—to stay and sin or to go and obey. What choice did he make? To go. He considered not the enjoyment of sin. To have sought to retain his place in the Egyptian court would have been sin.

It wasn't sin for Moses to be in the Egyptian court—until God told him to be somewhere else. It's not sin to have money or receive honors that the world gives unless you choose them over what God calls you to do. Sin can be fun for a season—but only a season.

1. Job 20:5—"The triumphing of the wicked is short, and the joy of the hypocrite but for a moment."

2. Job 21:7-13—Job complained to God, "Wherefore do the wicked live, become old, yea, are mighty in power?" Have you ever asked God why evil people sometimes fare better than you? "Their seed is established in their sight with them, and their offspring before their eyes. Their houses are safe from fear, neither is the rod of God upon them. Their bull gendereth, and faileth not; their cow calveth, and casteth not her calf [they don't have problems raising cattle]. They send forth their little ones like a flock, and their children dance [they have happy, healthy children]. They take the timbrel and harp, and rejoice at the sound of the flute. They spend their days in wealth, and in a moment go down to sheol." What a picture! Sin is pleasurable—for a while. But it's gone in a moment.

3. Psalm 73:12-19—"Behold, these are the ungodly, who prosper in the world; they increase in riches. Verily, I have cleansed my heart in vain, and washed my hands in innocence. For all the day long have I been plagued, and chastened every morning. If I say, I will speak thus; behold, I should offend against the generation of thy children. When I thought to know this, it was too painful for me, until I went into the sanctuary of God; then understood I their end. Surely, Thou didst set them in slippery places; thou castedst them down into destruc-

tion. How are they brought into desolation, as in a moment! They are utterly consumed with terrors."

4. Isaiah 21:4b—"The night of my pleasure hath he [God] turned into fear unto me."

5. James 5:5—"Ye have lived in pleasure on the earth, and been wanton [got your hands on everything you could get]; ye have nourished your hearts, as in a day of slaughter." James in effect says, "You nourished yourselves and did what you wanted and got fat and sassy as in a day of slaughter."

Judgment is coming, and it will come suddenly and swiftly. Moses knew that sin may be pleasurable, but it is brief. The highest and most lasting joy is to do what God says.

I believe David experienced pleasure with Bathsheba. But later on in his life he cried out, "My sin is ever before me" (Ps. 51:3b). The baby produced from his illicit relationship with Bathsheba died. His son Absalom rebelled against him and ended up dead.

The Lord gives us pleasure forevermore. Moses made a conscious choice to suffer affliction with the people of God rather than to enjoy the pleasures of sin for a season. That was an act of faith. God has called us all to holiness—to come apart from sin. It's not always easy because the world tempts us. But Moses believed God and said, "God, You want me to do what's right, and You'll honor me for it—so I'll do it."

If you *really* believe God, what are you going to do? Are you going to do what God says? God has your interest at heart. Satan doesn't care about you; he only wants to devour you (1 Pet. 5:8). If you believe God, you'll do two things: (1) you'll reject the world's prestige for the honor that only God can give, and (2) you'll reject the world's pleasure for the everlasting pleasure that only He can give.

Focusing on the Facts

1. Why was it important for the readers of the book of Hebrews to understand the importance of faith (see p. 106)?
2. True or false: The writer of Hebrews uses Old Testament illustrations to avoid the charge that salvation by faith is a new heresy (see p. 106).
3. What is one definition of spiritual maturity (see p. 107)?
4. How would you define the shield of faith (see p. 109)?
5. What was the basis of Moses' greatness (Heb. 11:24-25; see p. 110)?
6. What were two aspects of Moses' education (see pp. 110-11)?
7. How do the world's standards for evaluating greatness differ from God's (see pp. 113-14)?
8. Cite some passages that indicate that sin's pleasures are only temporary (see pp. 115-16).

Pondering the Principles

1. We learned in this chapter about an important decision Moses faced. Like Moses, we face decisions every day in our walks with the Lord. We grow in spiritual maturity by learning to make correct decisions. For us to do so, we need to have correct information on which to base those decisions. That information comes from the Word of God. Do you regularly memorize Scripture, filling your mind with the information necessary for you to make correct decisions in your life? Can you say with the psalmist, "Thy word have I hidden in mine heart, that I might not sin against thee" (Ps. 119:11)? If you have not already done so, begin a program of Scripture memorization this week.

2. Moses paid a price to identify with God's people—he had to forsake the wealth, power, and pleasures of the Egyptian royal palace. There are places in the world today where Christians pay a high price to identify with the Body of Christ. In many regions of the world, such as Eastern Europe, the Soviet Union, and some of the Muslim nations in the Middle East, those who let their faith in Christ be known are subject to harassment, the loss of their children, the loss of their jobs, imprisonment, or even death. Make a commitment to pray daily for your brothers

and sisters in Christ who are suffering for their faith in Christ. Consider writing to a missions group that works in those regions for names of specific individuals you can pray for and write to.

8
Things Faith Accepts and Rejects—Part 2

Outline

Introduction

Review
I. Things Faith Rejects (vv. 24-27)
 A. The World's Prestige (v. 24)
 B. The World's Pleasures (v. 25)
  1. Job 20:5
  2. Job 21:7-13
  3. Psalm 73:12-19
  4. Isaiah 21:4*b*
  5. James 5:5

Lesson
  6. Luke 12:19-20
 C. The World's Plenty (v. 26)
  1. "Esteeming"
  2. "The reproach of Christ"
   a) The problem
   b) The possible solutions
    (1) Moses is referring to himself
    (2) Moses was a picture of Christ
    (3) Moses bore the reproach of Messiah before He
     came
   c) The persecuted examples
    (1) David
    (2) Paul
    (3) Israel
    (4) All who serve Him
    (5) The church

Introduction

We saw in our last lesson that life is made up of decisions. From the time that we wake in the morning we begin a process of making decisions. We go through life making the decision to be filled with the Spirit or to quench Him—deciding for the will of God or against it. And when spiritual maturity comes, the decisions become less frequent because both of the wills agree.

In looking at the life of Moses, we are zeroing in on the decisions that faith makes. When somebody really believes and trusts that God has his best interests at heart, he will make certain decisions on the basis of that trust. Those decisions, then, govern his temporal as well as his eternal existence.

People throughout history have tried to reach God by everything but faith. They've tried to reach God by their own self-effort, their own works, their own invented legalistic codified systems, their own complicated ceremonies, and their own strange rituals. People have used all of these ways in their attempt to reach God—but they never succeed. Why? Because people can reach God only on the basis of simple belief. All God asks is that we believe Him; He does the work Himself. When Jesus died on the cross and said, "It is finished" (Gk., *tetelestai*), that's what He meant (John 19:30). When we apprehend salvation, it's only on the basis of His work and our faith—and our faith is a part of His work.

Having based the discussion of Hebrews 11 on the concept of faith, the writer of Hebrews moves to the life of Moses. Here we see what faith accepts and what it rejects.

Review

I. THINGS FAITH REJECTS (vv. 24-27)

A. The World's Prestige (v. 24; see pp. 110-14)

"By faith Moses, when he was come to years [forty years old], refused to be called the son of Pharaoh's daughter."

When Moses was forty he reached a crisis point in his life. He had to make the decision to either continue being a part of palace life with all the riches, honor, and prestige, or to turn his back on it, assign himself to the children of Israel, and become their deliverer from the bondage of Egypt, as God had asked. Faith that believes God makes the right decision and rejects the world's prestige. Moses refused one of the highest positions in his part of the world and, by faith, obeyed God (see pp. 110-16).

B. The World's Pleasures (v. 25; see pp. 114-16)

"Choosing rather to suffer affliction with the people of God than to enjoy the pleasures of sin for a season."

Sin is pleasurable—for a season. And when the season is over, sin bites and stings.

121

In our last lesson we looked at several passages illustrating this point (see pp. 115-16).

1. Job 20:5

2. Job 21:7-13

3. Psalm 73:12-19

4. Isaiah 21:4*b*

5. James 5:5

Lesson

6. Luke 12:19-20—"I will say to my soul, Soul, thou hast much goods laid up for many years; take thine ease. Eat, drink, and be merry. But God said unto him, Thou fool, this night thy soul shall be required of thee; then whose shall those things be, which thou hast provided?" Sin is pleasurable—for a while.

Moses chose to reject the pleasures of Egypt that could have been his if he had remained in the palace. Instead he decided to suffer affliction with the people of God. You may ask, "Why did he do that?" Because God told him to do it, and he believed God.

In our last lesson we talked about the fact that whenever a man believes God, he puts up the shield of faith and quenches the fiery darts of Satan. Sin occurs when a man believes Satan's lies instead of God's truth. Don't listen to Satan; he has been a liar from the very beginning. All he wants to do is ruin your life. Unfortunately, because of our depravity, we sometimes listen to Satan and do what he tells us to do. But when we listen to God and believe Him, sin will have no place in our lives.

The world's system must have looked alluring from Moses' vantage point, but he said no to it and chose to suffer affliction with the people of God. It's interesting that as Christians make this kind of choice to pull out from the world, they begin to realize, after a while, that the world doesn't matter much. The more you fall in love with Jesus Christ and the more that you set your life apart unto the things of God, the less all the world will mean to you. When your faith is directed toward God long enough, it will produce a life of joy. You will never want to forsake that joy to turn back toward the world. Moses was willing to do what God wanted him to do, even though it meant sacrificing the pleasures of the world.

Don't Expect the World to Understand

When a person forsakes the pleasures of the world to follow Christ, the world does not understand. They can't understand why a believer wants to go to church, read his Bible, sing hymns, and give to the church. The world does not understand why Christians restrict themselves from things they consider fun. It's tragic that the world views Christianity that way, but we can't expect them to understand until they see Christ.

First Peter 4:3 says, "For the time past of our life may suffice us to have wrought the will of the Gentiles." In other words, before we were saved we did whatever the world did. Verse 3 continues, "When we walked in lasciviousness [gross immoral indecency], lusts, excess of wine, revelings, carousings [Gk., *potoi*, "drinking parties"], and abominable idolatries." Verse 4 says, "In which they think it strange that ye run not with them." The world doesn't understand why we don't do those things.

God sets a new path, and by faith we go His way. Every once in a while we reject faith in God and go the other way, but it only brings hurt. If you live long enough in God's path and go the way God wants you to go, you'll find joy. Once you've tasted the joy that comes from Jesus Christ you realize that it's not worth giving up for what the world has to offer.

Moses made a conscious choice to suffer affliction. When we identify with Jesus Christ, we too will suffer affliction. When we confront the world, we receive resistance. Paul tells Timothy in 2 Timothy 3:12, "Yea, and all that will live godly in Christ Jesus shall suffer persecution." Like Moses, we too must make a conscious commitment that says, "I'm going God's way. I'm going to restrict some of the world's pleasures that are fun for a season and instead do what God wants so that in the long run my life can count for Him." The things we have to give up aren't worth having, anyway. A man can never give up anything for Jesus Christ, because whatever he could possibly yield will be replaced a millionfold by that which is valuable.

C. The World's Plenty (v. 26)

"Esteeming the reproach of Christ greater riches than the treasures in Egypt; for he had respect unto the recompense of the reward."

Moses could have had everything the world had to offer him. But the true man of faith doesn't want anything the world can offer. James 4:4 says, "Ye adulterers and adulteresses, know ye not that the friendship of the world is enmity with God? Whosoever, therefore, will be a friend of the world is the enemy of God." The world offers a lot; but if you live your life to gain the world's plenty, you're going to find yourself opposed to God.

1. "Esteeming"

In Greek the word *esteeming* literally means "to judge" or "to consider." It's a judicial word indicating that Moses did not make a quick decision or a rash conclusion. He laid it out, carefully considered it, and finally came to the conclusion that it's better to be reproached and to consider that reproach as riches than to have every treasure that the world has to offer.

2. "The reproach of Christ"

a) The problem

How could Moses esteem the reproach of Christ greater riches when Christ hadn't even been born?

b) The possible solutions

The word *Christ* (Gk., *Christos*) means "Messiah," and the word *Messiah* means "God's anointed one." This passage has several interpretations.

(1) Moses is referring to himself

It's possible that "Christ" in verse 26 shouldn't be translated with a capital C, but as "the anointed one" or "God's deliverer." In other words, Moses was saying that he was willing to suffer reproach as God's deliverer.

(2) Moses was a picture of Christ

This is perhaps closer to the truth than the previous solution. Moses was, in fact, a prefigure of Christ as the deliverer.

(3) Moses bore the reproach of Messiah before He came

I believe this is the most accurate. The world has been rejecting the Messiah since He came, and the world was not any different before He came. The world has always been against God and His deliverers. The reproach of the Messiah as it existed after Christ, in a spiritual sense existed before Christ was born.

c) The persecuted examples

(1) David—In Psalm 69:9*b* David says, "The reproaches of those who reproached thee are fallen upon me." When people persecute you, they are really persecuting Jesus Christ. When people are angry with you for your proclamation of faith, they're not after you—they're after Christ.

(2) Paul—In Galatians 6:17*b* Paul says, "I bear in my body the marks of the Lord Jesus." Paul was saying, "People keep beating me up for Christ's sake" (cf. 2 Cor. 12:10).

(3) Israel—The Messiah has always been identified with His people. When Israel suffered, Messiah suffered. In all their afflictions, He was afflicted.

(4) All who serve Him—Hebrews 13:13 says, "Let us go forth, therefore, unto him outside the camp, bearing his reproach." Everyone who has lined up with God by faith, lived for Him, and turned his back on the world's plenty has received the reproach that was directed against God. It belongs to all who serve Him.

(5) The church—Acts 5:41 says, "And they [the apostles] departed from the presence of the council, rejoicing that they were counted worthy to suffer shame for his name." Peter says in 1 Peter 4:14a, "If ye be reproached for the name of Christ, happy are ye."

3. "Greater riches than the treasures in Egypt"

   a) The wealth of Egypt

   Egypt was an extremely wealthy nation. The discovery of the tomb of Tutankhamen has produced some of the greatest treasures ever discovered in ancient Egypt. Moses, as a member of Pharaoh's court, had all of the wealth the world could offer. Yet he rejected it because he had faith in God's greater eternal riches. He must have realized the principle taught in Philippians 4:19: "My God shall supply all your need according to his riches in glory by Christ Jesus."

Which Is Better—to Be Given "Out of" or "According to" One's Riches?

Imagine you are destitute. You decide to go to a rich man for help. If the rich man writes a check for ten dollars, you'd say that he gave you out of his riches. But if this same man wrote you a check for one hundred thousand dollars, you'd say that he gave according to his riches. When Jesus gives, He doesn't give out of His riches; He gives according to His riches.

---

b) The wealth of God

(1) Psalm 37:16—"A little that a righteous man hath is better than the riches of many wicked."

(2) 1 Timothy 6:6-11—"Godliness with contentment is great gain; for we brought nothing into this world, and it is certain we can carry nothing out. And having food and raiment let us be therewith content. But they that will be rich fall into temptation and a snare." It's not a sin to be rich; it's a sin to *want* to be rich. If you work hard, do your best, use every faculty God has granted you, seek to glorify God in everything you do, and you get rich along the way—praise the Lord. But if your goal is to get rich you have the wrong motive. Verse 11 says, "But thou, O man of God, flee these things, and follow after righteousness, godliness, faith, love, patience, meekness." Make the goal of your life holiness. If God makes you rich along the way, that's wonderful. And if God keeps you poor, that's wonderful, too. What does it matter? God will supply your needs.

(3) Matthew 6:33—Jesus said, "But seek ye first the kingdom of God, and his righteousness, and all these things shall be added unto you."

It's not a question of how much you have; it's a question of what you really want in life. Attitude and motive are what is important in the Christian life.

4. "Respect unto the recompense of the reward"

When Moses rejected the world's prestige, pleasure, and plenty, did he crucify his dreams and wipe out all his hopes? No. He had his heart set on an eternal reward. That's what is meant at the end of verse 26. Moses had respect for the recompense of reward. His heart was set on eternal things. Faith knows that losing something worldly is not a loss. If you lay up treasure for yourself in heaven it's retained forever. Paul said, "For our light affliction, which is but for a moment, worketh for us a far more exceeding and eternal weight of glory" (2 Cor. 4:17). In Romans 8:17 Paul says that we are "joint heirs with Christ."

Faith doesn't want the world's prestige, and it doesn't care about the world's pleasure. It doesn't even care about the world's plenty.

D. The World's Pressure (v. 27)

"By faith he forsook Egypt, not fearing the wrath of the king; for he endured, as seeing him who is invisible."

Pharaoh was upset about Moses' leaving. Moses had tremendous pressure put on him, but he didn't let it get to him. He didn't fear the wrath of the king.

Satan tries to get believers to conform to the system. He uses all kinds of ways to accomplish his goal. For example, he uses the pressure of non-Christian friends who say, "What's the matter with you? Why don't you do what we do?" He uses the pressure of Christian friends who come along later and say, "The only way you can stay close to non-Christians so you can witness to them is to do what they do." If you conform to the world and rationalize that it's the only way to reach people for Christ, you've given in to Satan's pressure.

Satan also pressures believers to do dishonest things—tell small lies, fool around with the balance sheet, cheat on income tax. The pressure comes from all angles. Satan will continually try to pressure you to conform to the world. J. B. Phillips's New Testament translates Romans 12:2, "Don't let the world around you squeeze you into its own mold." That's what Satan wants to do.

What were the pressures Moses encountered?

1. The comfort of the palace

2. Pleasure

3. Riches

4. Honor

5. Debt (to Pharaoh's daughter)

6. Fear

Fear was probably the greatest pressure of all. Verse 27 says, "By faith he forsook Egypt, not *fearing* the wrath of the king" (emphasis added). The greatest pressure that Christians face in many cases is the pressure of fear. The reason that most Christians don't witness is because they're afraid. They're afraid of losing their popularity, becoming outcasts, not being accepted, or of offending somebody. It's all an ego fear. But Moses didn't fear. He forsook Egypt. The word *forsook* is the Greek verb *kata-leipo* and refers to a heart-renunciation. It wasn't just a physical moving away; it was a heart-renunciation. Moses chucked Egypt as a system and as a way of life. Satan uses fear to neutralize people, but it didn't neutralize Moses. However, it did work on many others in the Bible:

a) The victims

(1) Abraham was afraid and told a lie about Sarah

(2) Isaac was afraid and told a lie about Rebekah

(3) Jacob was afraid and fled from Laban

(4) Aaron was afraid, yielded to the people, and made a golden calf

(5) Israel was afraid to attempt the conquest of Canaan

(6) Twenty-two thousand members of Gideon's army were afraid and were disqualified

(7) David was afraid and ran from Absalom

(8) The disciples were afraid in a storm at sea

(9) Peter was afraid and denied Jesus

You and I have been afraid, and we've denied Christ in fear. Maybe you haven't stood up and rejected Christ verbally, but there are times you haven't said anything that could possibly connect you with Him.

Fear is a pressure. Many Christians melt at the threat of a loss of popularity or social status, or out of fear that people are going to cut them off, look down on them, call them fanatics, persecute them, and so on. The devil uses fear effectively, but it didn't work with Moses.

b) The victor

In Exodus 5 you can see how the devil attempted to pressure Moses. But Moses was bold, and the pressure didn't work. No matter what the pharaoh did or said, he didn't fear him. Moses gives us a great lesson on faith.

Faith doesn't fold under the world's pressure. Moses didn't fold because he saw "him who is invisible." He knew that no matter what happened, whatever he faced, he would be held up and strengthened.

Whenever you pass on an opportunity to confront people about Jesus Christ, it's because you're afraid. You're afraid because you don't trust the power of God. If you really trust Him, there wouldn't be anything to be afraid of. To be afraid means that you have stopped believing God, and when you stop believing God you forfeit faith. Faith says, "I'll believe God and reject the world's pressure." Unfortunately many Christians say, "I don't know if I can believe God at this point." That's the wrong decision. When we are afraid of the world and what people might say, we are exposing ourselves to condemnation for a gross lack of faith. Do you believe that God can do what He says He can do? People of faith have always believed God and not worried about others. Moses was like that.

Faith rejects the world's prestige, the world's pleasure, the world's plenty, and the world's pressure.

130

II. THINGS FAITH ACCEPTS (vv. 23, 28-29)

A. The Lord's Plans (v. 23)

"By faith Moses, when he was born, was hidden three months by his parents, because they saw he was a beautiful child, and they were not afraid of the king's commandment."

Pharaoh put out a decree that all male Hebrew babies were to be killed (Ex. 1:22). If a family didn't obey the order, they were subject to execution themselves. But that didn't bother Amram and Jochebed, Moses' parents. They hid Moses in their house for three months. They weren't afraid that the soldiers would find him and kill the whole family because they believed God and His plan regarding Moses.

1. Their revelation

Verse 23 says that Moses was "a beautiful child." In Acts 7:20 Stephen says that he was "exceedingly fair" (Gk., lit., "fair unto God"). In other words, God had especially set His affection on Moses. His parents didn't hide him because he was a handsome child; they hid him because God told them to. Scriptural faith is always in something that God has said. God told them that the child was fair unto Him and set apart for a specific purpose, so they hid him.

2. Their response

Amram and Jochebed could have sacrificed the infant and not risked their lives, but they were willing to do what God said. Without fear they took the child and kept him in the house for three months. We don't know why after three months they placed him in a boat on the river. He was probably too noisy and too hard to conceal. But for whatever reason, they laid him in a basket in the river. God must have told them about the destiny of the child, so they acted in faith, trusting God to protect him.

131

3. Their reward

It took faith to hide that little child for three months. It took faith to put that little child in the water. But God honored and rewarded their faith by bringing the baby back, giving Jochebed the privilege and joy of nursing, loving, cherishing, raising, and teaching him. She formed him into what he was, and taught him the messianic hope and the promise of Abraham. She was the one who taught him everything that was fulfilled in his own life as he led Israel.

It took tremendous faith to believe God as they hid the baby and then as they put him in the river. It took faith, but they obeyed God's plan. God has a plan, and His plan always works if you obey it. You don't need to try to help God re-organize it. Sarah tried to help God with a plan and produced a race of people who were a thorn in Israel's flesh from the very beginning. Don't try to help God; let Him work His plans. Only one thing is needed in the Christian life: obedience. God makes the plans, and we walk in them.

Moses' parents illustrate that the life of faith accepts God's plan.

B. The Lord's Provision (v. 28)

"Through faith he kept the passover, and the sprinkling of blood, lest he that destroyed the first-born should touch them."

Do you remember the last plague on Egypt? God in effect said, "All of the firstborn animals and sons are going to die. I'm going to come through the land with the angel of death and every firstborn in the land is going to die." Many people who heard didn't believe God. But Moses believed. Then God said, "There's going to be a provision for you, however, if you'll kill a lamb, take its blood, and put it on the doorposts. If you do that, the angel of death will pass by the house." Do you know who followed those instructions? The people who believed God. The Passover became a beautiful picture of the provision of the blood of Christ.

The judgment of God sweeps over civilization and passes by all those who are covered with the blood of Jesus Christ.

Moses believed God for His provision. Faith always accepts God's provision. Moses didn't say, "God, I've got a terrific idea of something You could add to that. What if we perform good deeds?" God made a provision, and Moses didn't add anything to it—he just did it! God has made a provision for the souls of people—the blood of Jesus Christ. Don't add anything to it—just accept it! When you receive Jesus Christ by faith, you've applied the blood of Christ. Romans 8:1 says, "There is, therefore, now no condemnation to them who are in Christ Jesus."

Faith accepts God's provision. That is the difference between faith and works. Works tries to make it on its own; faith says, "God did it—I believe it." Faith always accepts God's provision as well as God's plan.

C. The Lord's Promise (v. 29)

"By faith they passed through the Red Sea as by dry land, which the Egyptians, attempting to do, were drowned."

The Red Sea rolled up on both sides—hundreds and hundreds of feet deep. The people went down to the shore, and Moses said, "All right, we're going to cross." Someone probably said, "Oh, yeah? Who says it's going to stay up there?" Moses probably replied, "Who says it's going to stay? God says it's going to stay." The skeptic must have pondered this a moment then asked, "Could God do something to prove it?" God said to Moses, "Just reach out over the sea, and it will part." It did, but the people were afraid. However, they didn't have a choice. God prompted their faith with the Egyptian army. They either stayed and got massacred, or they moved on by faith. Faith takes God at His word and is victorious; but presumption drowns. The Egyptians presumed—and they drowned.

If you're waiting for a ferry to take you across the sea of your Christian life, it will never come. If you're waiting for calm water, it will never come. You're going to have to walk through the sea with it all piled up on both sides and believe God that it's going to stay there. The Christian life is a matter of believing God's promise. He says, "I'll hold everything up for you as you pass through the sea of this world." All we have to do is believe Him. That's the choice of faith. It believes God's plans, God's provision, and God's promise, and it rejects whatever the world has to offer.

Focusing on the Facts

1. Why does the world have a difficult time understanding Christians (see p. 123)?
2. What should Christians expect when they confront the world (2 Tim. 3:12; see pp. 123-24)?
3. True or false: Moses' decision to forsake the riches of Egypt and identify with God's people was made on the spur of the moment (see p. 124).
4. Explain how Moses could have considered the reproach of Christ greater riches than the treasures of Egypt when Christ had not yet been born (see pp. 124-25).
5. True or false: It is not a sin to be wealthy (see p. 127).
6. _____ and _____ are what really matter in the Christian life (see p. 127).
7. What did it mean for Moses to have "respect unto the recompense of the reward" (Heb. 11:26; see pp. 127-28)?
8. What are some of the ways Satan attempts to pressure us to conform to the world's system (see p. 128)?
9. What were some of the ways Satan tried to pressure Moses into conforming to the world system of his day (see pp. 128-29)?
10. What is the greatest pressure Satan uses to neutralize Christians (see p. 129)?
11. Why didn't Moses fold under the pressure he faced (see p. 130)?
12. What is the underlying cause of our fear of confronting the world (see p. 130)?
13. What motivated Moses' parents to risk their lives by hiding him (Heb. 11:23; see p. 131)?
14. In what way did God honor the faith of Moses' parents (see p. 132)?
15. The one thing needful in the Christian life is _____ (see p. 132).
16. Faith always accepts God's _____ (see p. 133).

Pondering the Principles

1. When Moses and the Israelites reached the shore of the Red Sea, they had to rely on God's promise that they could safely cross over—with no visible assurance that they could make it. Do you sometimes find it difficult to believe God's promises when there is no tangible evidence that they will be fulfilled? If so, memorize 2 Corinthians 5:7, and spend some time recalling the times in your life when God's promises have been fulfilled.

2. One of the greatest weapons Satan uses in his warfare against Christians is fear. Proverbs 29:25 tells us "the fear of man bringeth a snare." If you struggle with fear, use a concordance or topical Bible to do a topical study on fear. Some of the questions you may wish to answer are: What is proper fear? What is improper fear? What causes fear? What should we do when we are afraid?

9
The Pinnacle of Faith

Outline

Introduction

Review

Lesson
I. The Courage to Conquer in Struggle (vv. 30-35*a*)
  A. Joshua and the Children of Israel (v. 30)
    1. Their obstacles
      a) The walls
      b) The location
      c) The negative report
    2. Their order
    3. Their obedience
  B. Rahab (v. 31)
  C. Gideon (v. 32)
  D. Barak (v. 32)
  E. Samson (v. 32)
  F. Jephthah (v. 32)
  G. David (v. 32)
  H. Samuel (v. 32)
  I. The Prophets and Others (vv. 32*b*-35*a*)
II. The Courage to Continue in Suffering (vv. 35*b*-38)
III. The Courage to Count on Salvation (vv. 39-40)
  A. God's Promise (v. 39)
  B. God's Provision (v. 40)

Introduction

As we have been reminded several times in this study of Hebrews 11, the Holy Spirit is making a concentrated effort to extol the virtues of faith. He wants us to recognize the tremendous importance of a faith that is total. We have seen that this faith is defined as simply trusting completely and unconditionally in what God says, strictly on the basis that He said it.

Every man lives his life either believing in what God says and basing his life on it or in betting his life on his own attitudes, intellect, and understanding. Those are the only options. The faith that is talked about in this chapter is the faith that takes the bare Word of God and acts on it, simply because it is the Word of God—no other reason. True faith doesn't need to ask any questions. It is believing what God said simply because He's God and He said it—without any need for an explanation. In fact, true trust doesn't need explanations. That which looks for signs, wonders, and explanations is not faith—it's doubt looking around to see if it can find some proof. Often, to believe God is to do that which is unreasonable, illogical, and different than what the world would dictate; yet faith willingly obeys.

Review

We have been studying the lives of men who believed God's Word and didn't ask questions. We have looked at:

A. Abel—Abel didn't question God. God told him to make a sacrifice and how to do it, and Abel did so. He didn't ask for reasons.

B. Enoch—Enoch didn't question God. God said, "Enoch, separate yourself from the world and walk with Me," and he did so.

C. Noah—Noah didn't question God. He obeyed even though it seemed illogical to spend 120 years building a boat in the desert. Why did he do it? Because God told him to. That's all he needed.

D. Abraham—Abraham believed God. God said, "I want you to go to a land I'll show you, and I want to give you a promise that you'll never see fulfilled in your lifetime." Abraham got up and went. Why? Because God told him to go. He never asked a question; he just obeyed.

E. Isaac, Jacob, and Joseph—These men, against the natural course of human events, accepted God's Word without question and died in faith, never seeing the promise they hoped in. They died believing God would make good His promise.

F. Moses—Moses believed God. God told him to leave the pleasure and the plenty of Egypt and to go down and lead His people. Moses didn't question God; he immediately did what God said.

Why did these men commit themselves to God? Why did they believe God? It all boils down to the fact that they had a right view of who God is. The life of faith is based on proper theology. It may be difficult to do what God says; it may seem strange; it may cause suffering; it may separate you from people you love; it may cost you your ambitions and dreams; it may even cost you your life. But obeying God is what faith is all about. Faith, then, is based on a person's attitude toward God. The reason all these men of faith trusted God was because they had the right view of who He was. For example, Moses did what he did because he saw "him who is invisible" (Heb. 11:27b). He focused on God and His character.

These heroes of faith had such a lofty, exalted knowledge of the sovereign, loving, covenant-keeping, faithful God, that they took Him at His Word and banked their lives on it—even though it was often out of the ordinary and contrary to what their senses told them. They obeyed God simply because He said to. Your faith is based on your view of God. If your faith is inadequate, read your Bible and find out what kind of a God you have. That will increase your faith.

We've seen a lot about faith in Hebrews 11. We've seen the life of faith (Abel), the walk of faith (Enoch), the work of faith (Noah), the pattern of faith (Abraham), the victory of faith (Isaac, Jacob, and Joseph), and the choices of faith (Moses). Now we come to the pinnacle: the courage of faith. The true test of faith is courage. When faith is exhibited in the face of disaster, trial, and trouble, its legitimacy is proved.

In Hebrews 11:30-40 faith is seen at its highest point. Faith has the courage to do three things: to conquer in struggle, to continue in suffering, and to count on salvation.

Lesson

I. THE COURAGE TO CONQUER IN STRUGGLE (vv. 30-35*a*)

Life is a struggle for the believer. The only thing we have to challenge the struggles that face us is the faith that we have in God. This ability to conquer our circumstances is illustrated for us in verses 30-35*a*.

A. Joshua and the Children of Israel (v. 30)

"By faith the walls of Jericho fell down, after they were compassed about seven days" (cf. Josh. 6:1-20).

1. Their obstacles

a) The walls

The Greek word for "walls" used here is *teichos,* and it refers to the massive outer walls of the city. These walls were so wide that two chariots could run side by side along the top!

b) The location

Up to this point, the writer of Hebrews has been citing great examples of faith chronologically. Now he moves into the Promised Land, showing that the first obstacle the Israelites faced when they arrived in the land was Jericho. Jericho was a frontier fortress set up by the Canaanites to defend their land. It was just across the Jordan River in one of the bleakest parts of Israel. Its location was such that people coming across the Jordan River would be stopped immediately by its massive fortress.

140

c) The negative report

> Another obstacle that the Israelites faced was fear of
> the Canaanites. Their fear was based on a report they
> had received years earlier from some men that Moses
> had sent into Canaan to search out the land. They
> came back and in effect said, "Forget it! There's no
> way we can conquer this land. Those people are so
> big we look like grasshoppers next to them" (cf.
> Num. 13:33). This was terribly discouraging to them
> after hundreds of years waiting and forty years of
> roaming around the desert. Now Moses, their great
> leader, was dead, and things looked desperate. But
> Joshua led them across the Jordan River into the
> Promised Land where they came face to face with
> Jericho.

Jericho was their first major obstacle. The courage of
their faith was immediately tested. God had told them
He would give them the land, but I imagine some people looked at Jericho and said, "Sure, God's going to
give us the land. Here we are with no army—no nothing!" Here was a band of slaves that had roamed around
the desert for forty years facing a city that was walled,
barred, and fortified. It looked like an impossible task.
But Jericho was the gateway to the Promised Land, and
they had to conquer it. And they did. It didn't fall to battle; it fell to faith.

2. Their order

God told Joshua to have the people line up, walk
around the city once, and then go back to their camp.
They were to do this for six days in a row. On the seventh day they were to walk around the city seven times
and blow their horns and shout with a great shout.
When Joshua told the people the plan there must have
been a lot grumbling throughout the camp. It took a tremendous amount of faith to follow through with this
plan. Why? First, it was embarrassing. Second, the Canaanites could shoot at them or drop rocks on them from
the top of the wall. The plan appeared ridiculous. If you
imagine it was tough the first day, imagine how hard it

must have been about the fifth or six day. But they obeyed.

3. Their obedience

The Israelites were unprotected in the desert, sandwiched between the Jordan River and the city of Jericho. They had nowhere to go. When they crossed the Jordan they burned their bridges behind them. They were cut off from escape with no homes to retreat to or fortresses for defense. They had to live on faith. The only way to go was forward, even though the obstacle was so massive that it looked hopeless. But they believed God, marched around the city once a day for six days and seven times on the seventh day—then they shouted. It took great faith to shout. But they shouted at the top of their voices and the walls of the city collapsed. That's how faith operates. Faith conquers the obstacle because it believes God. When God says, "I'll do it this way," faith says, "If You said it, You'll do it."

The faith of Joshua and the children of Israel serves as a good illustration of the Christian life. A Christian is never going to live the Christian life without running into some Jericho—some massive problem. But it's a trifle to the almighty God and will fall into ashes before faith. Whatever your Jericho is, believe God for its collapse.

B. Rahab (v. 31)

"By faith the harlot, Rahab, perished not with them that believed not, when she had received the spies with peace."

1. Her background

Isn't it interesting that a prostitute found her way into the hall of fame with the heroes of faith? There's one thing for sure—she wasn't saved by her works! Not only was she a prostitute, but she was a Gentile—a Canaanite. Worse than that she was an Amorite, a member of a race that God had devoted to destruction—but that's how God's grace works! His mercy is open to all who will receive it. Even in the Old Testament, God's grace was always wider than Israel.

Verse 31 refers to "them that believed not." Who is that? The whole city of Jericho. What didn't they believe? They didn't believe the word of the Lord. You may ask, "Do you mean they heard the word of the Lord?" Of course. They knew God had given the land to the children of Israel. I don't know how they got the message, but they did. Why do I say that? Because verse 31 says that they "believed not." The Greek word used here is *apeitheo*, which means "to be disobedient." For them to be disobedient means that they heard a command and didn't obey it. I believe God told them that the land was for Israel and that He was going to destroy them, but that all those who turned to Him in mercy would be set free. They didn't believe it, so they were wiped out.

The Canaanites were a debauched people. History tells us that when they built buildings they put live babies in jars and built them into the walls. They were involved in all kinds of orgies and atrocities. God punished that city.

2. Her belief

God spared one woman who believed and the members of her family who were in her house. Verse 31 says that she "had received the spies with peace." The Greek word used here is *dechomai*, which means "to welcome with hospitality." The record of this incident is in Joshua 2 and 6. Joshua sent two spies into the land to search it out before they crossed over the Jordan River. They ended up in Rahab's house in the city of Jericho. While they were there, the king of Jericho heard that there were two Israelite spies in Rahab's house, so he sent some men to capture them. When the soldiers arrived, Rahab hid the two spies, sent the soldiers on a wild goose chase, and then provided for the spies' safe escape.

The reason she did that is found in Joshua 2:9-11. She said to the two spies, "I know that the Lord hath given you the land, and that your terror is fallen upon us, and that all the inhabitants of the land faint because of you. For we have heard how the Lord dried up the water of the Red Sea for you, when ye came out of Egypt; and what ye did unto the two kings of the Amorites, who were on the other side of the Jordan, Sihon and Og, whom ye utterly destroyed. And as soon as we had heard these things, our hearts did melt, neither did there remain any more courage in any man, because of you; for the Lord your God, He is God in heaven above, and in earth beneath."

Rahab put her faith in the true God and believed God's word. That took courage, because there wasn't a chance in a million, physically speaking, that those children of Israel could defeat Jericho. But she staked her life on the fact that God had said they would—and she wanted to be on God's side. It took courageous faith to hide those spies, because she could have been killed for doing so. And it also took faith to believe those spies. How did she know that they would keep their promise? She had great courage.

3. Her blessing

God honored that prostitute in Jericho. First, He honored her with salvation. Second, He honored her by placing her in the messianic line. Rahab became the mother of Boaz, who became the husband of Ruth, the great-great-grandmother of David. Rahab the harlot was in the messianic line. That's God's grace!

C. Gideon (v. 32)

The story of Gideon is recorded in Judges 7. Gideon was a judge who ruled in Israel. God had given him the commission of wiping out the Midianites who had an army of 135,000 (cf. Judg. 8:10). Gideon formed an army of 32,000 men. God said, "That's too many. Cut it down." When God was through paring down Gideon's army, there were 300 men left. And they weren't chosen by determining who was the best wrestler, or the strongest, or the most accurate with weapons—they were chosen by the way they drank water!

Once Gideon had his army of 300, the Lord told him to take these men and surround the camp of the Midianites (which would be quite a task for 300 men). Then He told Gideon to have each of his men take a torch, a pitcher, and a trumpet as their "weapons." God said, "Just stand on the hillside surrounding the valley where the Midianites are, blow your horns, smash your pitchers, and all the Midianites will run around and kill each other." And that happened. The Midianites who panicked and killed each other numbered 120,000, and the 15,000 that were left fled.

It took faith to do what Gideon did, but he believed God. He tackled something that someone couldn't tackle without faith in God. Faith has courage to conquer in struggle—no enemy is too great.

D. Barak (v. 32)

The story of Barak is in Judges 4. Barak took ten thousand men and was assigned the task of fighting against the mighty and massive force of Sisera, commander-in-chief of the confederate chariot force of the Canaanites. The odds were incredible. Practically speaking there was no way Barak could handle Sisera. But Deborah, a prophetess and judge of Israel, came to Barak and told him that God would give him victory over the Canaanites. Barak believed God, gathered his army together, and went to battle. If he hadn't believed God, he would have been foolish to do what he did. But he believed God and won the battle.

E. Samson (v. 32)

If you go back and read Judges 13-16, you'll see that Samson was a man of great faith. He knew he had power, but he also knew that the source of his power was God. He believed God and trusted Him to supply the power he needed. He slew a lion bare-handed (Judg. 14:5-6). God called Samson to be the champion of Israel against the Philistines. In spite of the terrible tragedy of his life with Delilah, his life still stands out as a great life of faith. He never feared the enemy because he knew God was faithful. For example:

1. Judges 15:1-5—He burned the Philistines' crops.

2. Judges 15:6-8—He "smote . . . with a great slaughter" the Philistines who killed his wife and father-in-law.

3. Judges 15:14-16—He slew one thousand Philistines with the jawbone of an ass.

4. Judges 16:2-3—When the people of Gaza tried to trap him inside the city, he just picked up the gates, the side posts, and the beam across the top, and carried them up a mountain.

5. Judges 16:25-30—His last conquest of faith was when, as a blinded prisoner, he pulled down a monstrous Philistine temple where he was held captive, killing more Philistines by his death than he had killed in his lifetime.

According to Judges 13:5, Samson knew that God had called him to conquer the Philistines. He believed God and never faced the Philistine army without absolute courage in the fact that God had promised to give him the power.

It's tragic that so many Christians talk about faith, but they don't have enough courage to face their battles with the belief that God will give them the victory. Instead, they hang back waiting for reinforcements.

F. Jephthah (v. 32)

In Judges 11:32-33 we see the courage of Jephthah, who faced tremendous odds yet believed God and won the victory.

G. David (v. 32)

David spent his whole life facing incredible odds. It all began when he fought Goliath. There seemed no way that a boy such as David could have victory over a gigantic, experienced warrior like Goliath—but David believed God. He said to Goliath, "This day will the Lord deliver thee into mine hand; and I will smite thee, and take thine head from thee; and I will give the carcasses of the host of the Philistines this day unto the fowls of the air, and to the wild beasts of the earth, that all the earth may know that there is a God in Israel" (1 Sam. 17:46). Where did he get that kind of courage? He believed God.

H. Samuel (v. 32)

Samuel was a great man of faith. He never fought in a war, but he fought the battle of idolatry and immorality. He had to stand up in the midst of a polluted society and speak the truth. He had to stand for the courage of his convictions when all of the people were immoral.

I. The Prophets and Others (vv. 32b-35a)

Here is a description of the prophets, from Samuel to John the Baptist, who courageously and confidently accepted God's commands, standing alone, face to face with apparently undefeatable hostile hordes for the sake of obedience to God. In every case they and other men and women of faith were victorious. Verses 33-35a say that they through faith:

1. "Subdued kingdoms"—The Greek word for "subdued" is *katagonizomai* and means "to fight down" or "to overcome." They were victorious.

2. "Wrought righteousness"—The Greek literally means they executed justice. It refers to leaders who upheld justice against pressures (cf. 2 Sam. 8:15).

3. "Obtained promises"—God gave all the prophets promises and told them He'd give them victory. They obeyed and obtained victory.

4. "Stopped the mouths of lions"—This obviously refers to Daniel, who obeyed God even though it meant being thrown into a den of lions. Because he believed God, God protected him (Dan. 6:16-22).

5. "Quenched the violence of fire"—This refers to Daniel's three Hebrew friends—Shadrach, Meschach, and Abednego—who were thrown into fiery furnace because they believed God and refused to worship the statue of the king (Dan. 3:8-28).

6. "Escaped the edge of the sword"—David escaped the sword of Goliath and Saul—and there are many other examples.

7. "Out of weakness were made strong"—God promised David that as long as he and his descendants remained faithful, obedient, and righteous, there would always be a line of sons on the throne (1 Kings 2:4). King Hezekiah was about to die, and he did not have a son. He recalled God's promise of 1 Kings 2:4, and he began to pray for an heir to the throne. God kept His promise, and Hezekiah became well, lived fifteen years, and fathered a son (cf. 2 Kings 20:1-6, 21; 21:1).

8. "Received their dead raised to life again"—Elijah raised the dead son of the widow of Zarephath (1 Kings 17:17-24). Elisha raised the dead son of the Shunammite wom-

148

an (2 Kings 4:18-37). The faith of both these prophets brought back those children from the dead.

II. THE COURAGE TO CONTINUE IN SUFFERING (vv. 35b-38)

Sometimes God doesn't design the battle to be victorious. Sometimes He designs it to go on and on. The second characteristic of courageous faith is that it continues in suffering. Faith that conquers is great faith, but faith that continues in suffering is even greater. That kind of faith continues in suffering without murmuring and believes God. Illustrations of this faith start in verse 35b:

A. "Others were tortured"—The Greek word for "tortured" is *tumpaizō* and literally means "to torture with the tympanum." A tympanum was a wheel-shaped frame over which criminals were stretched and then beaten with clubs.

B. "Not accepting deliverance"—These people could have recanted their faith and denied God, and they would have been delivered. But they suffered instead.

C. "That they might obtain a better resurrection"—What gave them the courage to stand and not deny their faith? They had their eyes on something glorious in the future. They never sacrificed the future on the altar of the immediate. They wanted the fullness of their reward, so they endured torture.

D. "And others had trial of cruel mockings"—Sometimes the hardest pressure that comes against us is mental pain, the anguish of being criticized. Jeremiah went through this kind of pressure (Jer. 20:7; cf. 2 Kings 2:23; 2 Chron. 36:16).

E. "And scourgings"—These were lashings with brutal whips. Jeremiah experienced scourging as well (Jer. 20:2).

F. "Of bonds and imprisonment"—Some examples of people who were bound and imprisoned are Joseph (Gen. 39:20), Micaiah (1 Kings 22:27), Hanani (2 Chron. 16:10), and Jeremiah (Jer. 20:2; 37:15; 38:6).

G. "They were stoned"—An Old Testament man of faith who was stoned was Zechariah (2 Chron. 24:20-22).

H. "They were sawn asunder"—Tradition tells us that Isaiah was sawed in half.

I. "Were tested"—It's hard to know exactly what this means, but perhaps it's best explained if it refers to the torture of being pressured to deny God. They were tested—almost to the point of breaking—to deny God.

J. "Were slain with the sword"—The literal Greek says that they "died by sword-slaughter." Some of the faithful in the Old Testament were slaughtered because they wouldn't deny God.

K. "They wandered about in sheepskins and goatskins; being destitute, afflicted, tormented. . . . They wandered in deserts, and in mountains, and in dens and caves of the earth"—In other words, they were poor. Because of their belief in God, some of them had to forsake everything the world had to offer. They lived in poverty. The only clothing they could afford to wear was sheepskins and goatskins.

L. "Of whom the world was not worthy"—The terrible suffering that came to the people of God was met with faith and courage, and the world wasn't worthy of them. The world thought that the people of God were unworthy to live in the world; but the fact of the matter was that they were so worthy they shouldn't have even been in the world at all. God will make up for their treatment in heaven. They'll be worthy of everything they receive there.

In Romans 8:18 Paul says, "For I reckon that the sufferings of this present time are not worthy to be compared with the glory which shall be revealed in us." Peter says in 1 Peter 1:3-4, "Blessed be the God and Father of our Lord Jesus Christ, who, according to His abundant mercy, hath begotten us again unto a living hope by the resurrection of Jesus Christ from the dead, to an inheritance incorruptible, and undefiled, and that fadeth not away, reserved in heaven for you." Can't you imagine some of those suffering believers in Peter's day who were rejoicing about what was going to be theirs? This world isn't worthy of people who have the courage of faith to suffer for Christ. That is the pinnacle of faith—to endure trials with courage and faith in God and never waver.

III. THE COURAGE TO COUNT ON SALVATION (vv. 39-40)

A. God's Promise (v. 39)

"These all, having received witness through faith, received not the promise."

Everyone from Abel to Samuel had to live on hope. They believed that God would redeem and reward them someday when all the suffering was over. What is the promise referred to in verse 39? It's not the promise of the land, because that promise was never given to Abel and Enoch. What was promised that none of these heroes of faith received? The promise of a Redeemer, the promise of Messiah, the promise of a covenant that could bring perfection, the promise of a salvation that could bring men into God's presence totally and fully. They never knew the Messiah, but they believed He would come.

First Peter 1:10-11 says, "As to this salvation, the prophets who prophesied of the grace that would come to you made careful search and inquiry, seeking to know what person or time the Spirit of Christ within them was indicating as He predicted the sufferings of Christ and the glories to follow" (NASB). In other words, they were looking to see when and how the Redeemer would come. In the midst of all their suffering, they were the courageous ones who counted on salvation. They believed God for His promise of full, final salvation, but they didn't receive it.

B. God's Provision (v. 40)

"God having provided some better thing for us, that they without us should not be made perfect."

What is the "better thing" in the book of Hebrews? The New Covenant. They never found the promise in the Old Covenant. They never found the perfect High Priest because their priests kept dying. But God provided a better

151

thing for us, "that they without us should not be made perfect." In other words, their perfection had to wait for us. The New Covenant gave them what the Old Covenant couldn't give.

All these lived by faith—a courageous faith. So courageous was their faith, they conquered in struggle, they continued in suffering, and they counted on salvation to come. They never saw it, but they believed God and received it on credit. The world wasn't worthy of these people—I pray that we would live the kind of lives that it might be said of us, "This world isn't worthy of them!"

Focusing on the Facts

1. The life of faith is based on proper _____ (see p. 139).
2. Name three obstacles the Israelites encountered upon entering the Promised Land (see pp. 140-41).
3. In what way is the faith Joshua and the Israelites exhibited at Jericho an illustration of the Christian life (see p. 143)?
4. True or false: In the Old Testament, God's grace was limited to Israel (see p. 143).
5. True or false: The inhabitants of Jericho were judged because of their failure to obey God's Word (see pp. 143-44).
6. Explain why Rahab was willing to help the two spies escape (Josh. 2:9-11; see p. 144).
7. True or false: God honored Rahab's faith by placing her into the messianic line (see p. 145).
8. How was Gideon's faith manifested (see p. 145)?
9. What was the source of Samson's courage (see pp. 146-47)?
10. Cite some examples of the faith of the prophets (see pp. 147-49).
11. What gave courage to those who suffered for their faith (see p. 149)?

Pondering the Principles

1. One of the reasons the great men of faith we've been studying had such strong faith is that they had an exalted view of God.

Our faith can be no stronger than our knowledge of God. If you struggle with weak faith, perhaps it is because you don't know your God as well as you might. Why not get to know God better by studying His attributes? The following books can help you in your study: *The Knowledge of the Holy,* by A. W. Tozer, *Knowing God,* by J. I. Packer, and *The Existence and Attributes of God,* by Stephen Charnock.

2. As we learn from this chapter, the life of faith isn't always easy. Many of the heroes of the faith suffered persecution, deprivation, or martyrdom. Knowing this, do not be surprised when trials come your way, but expect them as a normal part of the life of faith. Meditate on the following verses to prepare yourself to face your next trial: Acts 14:22, Romans 8:18, 1 Corinthians 10:13, Philippians 1:29-30, James 1:2-4, and 1 Peter 2:20-21, 5:10.

10
Running the Race That Is Set Before Us

Outline

Introduction

Lesson
I. The Event (v. 1*c*)
   A. The Participants
      1. Whom does the "us" refer to in the book of Hebrews?
         a) Genuinely saved Jews who were beginning to fall back into Judaism
         b) Jews who were intellectually convinced that Jesus was the Messiah but hesitant to make the commitment
         c) Antagonistic Jews who weren't convinced or saved
      2. Whom does the "us" refer to in Hebrews 12:1?
         a) Primarily
         b) Secondarily
   B. The Pace
   C. The Preparation
      1. 1 Corinthians 9:24-25
      2. 2 Timothy 2:3-4
II. The Encouragement (v. 1*a*)
   A. The Witnesses
   B. The Testimony
III. The Encumbrances (v. 1*b*)
   A. The Weight
   B. The Sin
IV. The Example (v. 2*a*)
   A. His Faith
   B. Our Focus
V. The End (v. 2*b*)
VI. The Exhortation (vv. 3-4)

Introduction

Hebrews 12:1-4 says, "Wherefore, seeing we also are compassed about with so great a cloud of witnesses, let us lay aside every weight, and the sin which doth so easily beset us, and let us run with patience the race that is set before us, looking unto Jesus, the author and finisher of our faith, who for the joy that was set before him endured the cross, despising the shame, and is set down at the right hand of the throne of God. For consider him that endured such contradiction of sinners against himself, lest ye be wearied and faint in your minds. Ye have not resisted unto blood, striving against sin."

We have a figure of speech in this text. Good teaching comes down to the effective use of figures of speech. In the New Testament the Holy Spirit communicates many principles through figures of speech:

A. Warfare (2 Tim. 2:3; Eph. 6:10-17)

B. A Wrestling Match (Eph. 6:12)

C. A Boxing Match (1 Cor. 9:26; 2 Tim. 4:7a)

D. Slavery (Gal. 6:17; Rom. 1:1)

E. A Farming Operation (2 Tim. 2:6)

F. A Marriage (Rom. 7:4)

G. A Father/Son Relationship (Rom. 8:14-17; Heb. 12:6-7; 1 John 3:1-2)

H. A Race (1 Cor. 9:24-27; Gal. 5:7; Phil. 2:16; 3:13-14; 2 Tim. 4:7b)

The Christian life, then, is likened to many things; but our text in Hebrews 12:1-4 brings us to discuss the metaphor of a race. In order to break down the passage, we will consider several aspects of the Christian race: the event, the encouragement, the encumbrances, the example, the end, and the exhortation.

I. THE EVENT (v. 1c)

"Let us run with patience the race that is set before us."

A. The Participants

1. Whom does the "us" refer to in the book of Hebrews?

Basically it's a question of whether the writer of Hebrews is referring to Christians or Jews. In most cases, it is the broadest interpretation and refers to all those readers who are of a Jewish heritage. There's no doubt in my mind that the author of the book of Hebrews was Jewish. I don't know who the writer was, but he was Jewish. There is also no doubt that he was writing to Jews, because the book is addressed to the Hebrews. The whole analogy of the book is built on an understanding of Judaism, and the writer is commonly referring to his readers in the sense of their Jewishness rather than in the sense of their Christianity. The writer of Hebrews calls the Jewish readers "brethren." But when he wants to distinguish the Christians, he calls them "holy brethren." The words *brethren* and *us* can encompass the total Jewish audience to whom the writer is speaking.

When the author says, "Let us run with patience the race"—and the "us" refers to the broadest possible interpretation of his readers—we must understand who his readers are. They fall into three categories:

a) Genuinely saved Jews who were beginning to fall back into Judaism

These Jewish Christians began to experience tremendous pressure from their Jewish friends and family, and they began to waver. Even though they were saved, they started to go back to old customs, keep some of the feasts, make sacrifices, hang around the priests, and go back to the Temple standards. They began to fall back into Judaistic patterns to get some social acceptance—even though they were saved. The book of Hebrews is written primarily to these Jewish Christians, to tell them not to fall back into their old patterns of Judaism but to take their stand for Christ. Throughout the book the author says, "You have a better covenant and a better priest from a better priesthood with a better sacrifice that constitutes a better offering with better results." That is the main thrust of the book.

b) Jews who were intellectually convinced that Jesus was the Messiah but were hesitant to make the commitment

This second group of Jews was intellectually convinced that the gospel was true and that Jesus was the Messiah, but they never received Christ. They stayed on the fence, afraid to go over to the side of Christ because of what they saw happening to the ones who did. They saw Jewish believers being alienated from their society, ostracized from their Jewish heritage, turned into outcasts and traitors, and so on. They were hesitant to make a commitment. Periodic warnings to these Jews dot the book. These warnings frequently begin with the phrase "let us" (cf. 4:1, 11, 14, 16; 6:1; 10:22-23). Normally when the phrase "let us" is used in Hebrews, it is a call to this second category of Jewish people who were intellectually convinced that the gospel is true but wouldn't make the commitment for personal reasons.

c) Antagonistic Jews who weren't convinced or saved

These Jews compose the third category of readers.

2. Whom does the "us" refer to in Hebrews 12:1?

a) Primarily

Primarily it refers to those Jews who are intellectually convinced. He's saying, "Look, you must come to Christ. Get in the race. The Christian life is a race,

158

and you must be in it. You have to be on the track participating.''

b) Secondarily

Secondarily he is saying to the Christians, "If you're in the race, run it!" There were a lot of Christians who needed to get going.

Primarily he is inviting people to make a commitment to Christ, but there is also a secondary injunction to believers.

Are You Sitting on the Fence?

It's easy for people to sit on the fence. There are people that come to church who hear the Word of God and are intellectually convinced that it's true. Some of these people have probably had many of their doubts removed as they read literature defending Christianity. Perhaps they have counseled with people and talked with their friends, and they know it's true, but for some reason they won't get into the race. Maybe it's because they're afraid they're going to lose their friends, or they're afraid they're going to have to give up the person they're living with, or they're afraid of the moral consequences, or they realize that if they make a commitment to Christ they're going to have to clean up their lives. But for some reason—whatever it might be—there are people sitting on the fence. The Word of the Holy Spirit says to these people, "Get in the race!"

B. The Pace

We are called to run a race. Notice the word *race* in verse 1. It is the Greek word *agōn* from which we get the word *agony*.

The word *agōn* doesn't refer to spirit. There are many 100-yard-dash Christians. They sprint, then they flop. Then they go to a seminar, and off they go again. After that's worn off, they hear a great sermon, and they're off running again. This is not the kind of race that is talked about here. He's talking about a marathon; and he says this marathon is to be run with *hupomonē*, which means "endurance." This is an endurance race, not a short sprint. The Christian life is a commitment to run—with endurance—to victory.

C. The Preparation

To run the race with endurance demands discipline, rigid care, self-sacrifice, and self-denial. The Christian life is not one of passive luxury. We're not to ride around on flowery beds of ease. There must be a strenuous self-sacrifice that demands hard training and discipline. It isn't easy to be a Christian. It's the life of a soldier. Paul said at the end of his life, "I have fought a good fight, I have finished the course" (2 Tim. 4:7a). There must be a sense of commitment and discipline. Amos said, "Woe to them who are at ease" (Amos 6:1a). That's not a good place to be. There ought to be an aggressiveness to the Christian life. There ought to be a competitiveness to the Christian life insofar as we fight against weakness, indolence, laziness, ignorance, and sin to be what God wants us to be.

If you're not in the race, come to Christ, get over the fence, and get in the race. Once you're in it—run it! God doesn't want Christians lying around the track, confusing the issue. Remember, this is a race of endurance that requires disciplined training.

1. 1 Corinthians 9:24-25—Verse 24 says, "Know ye not that they who run in a race run all, but one receiveth the prize? So run, that ye may obtain." I get upset when I see Christians who don't want to win, who aren't working to the best of their ability to be the most excellent they can be. If you're a Sunday school teacher, be the most excellent teacher you can be. If you're leading a Bible study, run it to win. If you're a homemaker, be the most excellent you can be. If you're on the job, give the most excellent work you can give. That's the only way to live the Christian life. It takes discipline, but we must demand excellence of ourselves and run the race to win.

Paul continues in verse 25, "Every man that striveth for the mastery is temperate in all things." This means he doesn't have any indulgence, never breaks the training rules. You have to be able to say no to some things and cut yourself off from the world and the flesh. It's unbelievable how hard athletes train. But Paul says, "Now they do it to obtain a corruptible crown [a laurel wreath on the head], but we, an incorruptible." Our commitment should be much greater.

Pastors sometimes ask me, "How can you study the Bible four to six hours a day?" There are plenty of athletes who train four to six hours a day to attain what they want to attain, and I believe that the kingdom of God is infinitely more important. In fact, I should give more than an athlete, because God is seeking excellence.

2. 2 Timothy 2:3-4—"Thou, therefore, endure hardness, as a good soldier of Jesus Christ. No man that warreth entangleth himself with the affairs of this life." When a man is accepted into the army, he has time to get ready, but then once he's in the army, that's all he is—in the army and nothing else. Why? Because the army wants to be successful. And so it is that we must commit ourselves to excellence and to winning.

II. THE ENCOURAGEMENT (v. 1a)

"Wherefore, seeing we also are compassed about with so great a cloud of witnesses."

When I was a boy I heard someone preach on this passage. He said, "All the Old Testament saints up in heaven are watching you. It's like you're in a big stadium running your race, and they're sitting in the stands watching you. That is the 'cloud of witnesses' around us." The more I studied the Bible the more ridiculous that view became. People who have gone to heaven aren't interested in looking at me; they're fixing their gaze on the wonders of heaven. This verse is an encouragement to run, and the "cloud of witnesses" refers to the people who have testified that running the race is worthwhile.

A. The Witnesses

Look at the "wherefore" at the beginning of verse 1. It's there to take us backwards to chapter 11. What do we have there? A list of people who lived by faith: Abel, Enoch, Noah, Abraham, Isaac, Jacob, Joseph, Moses' parents, Moses, Joshua and Israel, Rahab, Gideon, Barak, Samson, Jephthah, David, Samuel, and the prophets. These are the witnesses.

B. The Testimony

What are the witnesses of chapter 11 saying? They're saying that the life of faith is the life that wins. They ran through lions' dens, through swords, through wars, through persecution, through crisis after crisis. It is the life of faith that wins, and they are living witnesses to the fact that we can run the race with endurance and know that God will honor us in the end. They ran the race and are witnesses to the victory. This mass of people or "cloud of witnesses" says to us, "Run the life of faith!"

Hebrews 12:1-2 is the continuation of chapter 11. It is an exhortation based on everybody else's life of faith—how they ran by faith in God and went right through the crisis to victory. So should we run the race on the testimony of these witnesses.

The examples of faith in chapter 11 put their trust in God, and God came through. The writer of Hebrews is saying to the Hebrew people, "If you haven't put your faith in Jesus Christ and you're hanging on the fence, let me remind you of the history of your ancestors who lived their lives by faith and went through crises with a sense of great victory." In other words, he's telling them to put their trust in God because He'll always come through. What is the proof? The heroes of faith in chapter 11.

The times when we feel our weaknesses and the times when we have our doubts are the times we need to look back at the lives of people whom God—because they ran the race with patience and endurance—honored and gave victory. That encourages me, because the God of yesterday is the God of today (Heb. 13:8), and He will give us the same victory.

III. THE ENCUMBRANCES (v. 1b)

"Let us lay aside every weight, and the sin which doth so easily beset us."

When you learn to run you have to learn to run light. You may train in a sweatsuit with weights on, but when you get to the race you take them off. You get rid of the bulk and run with the bare minimum. In the race of faith we need to strip off anything that will hold us back. What is the weight that holds us back?

A. The Weight

Many things can weigh us down and encumber us in the Christian life. Things such as materialism, sexual immorality, and ambition weigh us down in the race, but I believe the writer of Hebrews has something else in mind. What was the biggest weight that encumbered a Jew from coming to Christ? Legalism. Dead works characterized those Jewish believers. He told them to get in the race and run; but they were trying to run with all of their legalism, ceremonies, rituals and rites, and rules they had kept from Judaism. He was saying, "Get rid of all that and run the race of faith. Live by faith, not works."

Many Christians live by works. They believe that if they do certain things God will say, "That's wonderful. You went to a Bible study, read your Bible, and went to church"—as if God keeps a tally of every good work they do. God does not say, "If you have your morning devotions, you're going to be a good Christian." Unfortunately, there are a lot of Christians who think that way. They believe that if they go to church every Sunday and if they're kind to their neighbors they are good Christians. Those are good things, but they won't secure anyone spiritually. If those things are done in the overflow of one's love for Jesus Christ as an act of devotion, that's great. But there are many Christians depending on their good works. Instead of Jewish legalism it's Christian legalism.

B. The Sin

The second encumbrance mentioned in verse 1 is "the sin which doth so easily beset us." What is that sin? Doubt. You may say, "God, You can supply all my needs," but if you get nervous every time something doesn't go the way it should, you're doubting.

What is our protection against doubt? Paul says in Ephesians 6:16, "Above all, taking the shield of faith, with which ye shall be able to quench all the fiery darts of the wicked."

The large Roman shield called the *thureon* in Greek was four-and-a-half feet by two-and-a-half feet and was covered with thick leather soaked in oil. Any flaming arrows that sank into this leather would be extinguished. The shield of the Christian is faith. When Satan fires his temptations we stop them in the shield of faith. In other words, we say, "Satan, you're a big liar; nothing you say is true. Everything God says is true, so I'm going to believe God."

Every time you sin you believe Satan instead of God. When Satan came to Jesus in the wilderness, Jesus believed God and was without sin. Every sin is an act of unbelief. The one sin that besets the race of faith is doubt—believing the adversary rather than God.

The writer of Hebrews in effect says, "Get rid of your legalism and your doubt and run this race with confidence, realizing that a great cloud of witnesses lived the same life of faith, ran the same race, and was triumphant."

IV. THE EXAMPLE (v. 2a)

"Looking unto Jesus, the author and finisher of our faith."

A. His Faith

Christ is the greatest example of faith that ever lived. Philippians 2:6b-8 says that Christ "thought it not robbery [lit., "something to hold on to"] to be equal with God, but made himself of no reputation, and took upon him the form of a servant, and was made in the likeness of men; and, being

164

found in fashion as a man, he humbled himself and became obedient unto death, even the death of the cross." Jesus became a servant and believed God, who said He would not let His holy One see corruption (Ps. 16:10). Christ came into the world and died on the cross, knowing full well that even though He bore the sins of the world He would come out of the grave to be the Redeemer and be restored to the place He had with the Father before the world began. He believed the Father absolutely and totally, and His act of faith is unsurpassed. God became man, bore sin, and died in the confidence that He would be raised by the Father and exalted again. He was. And the reason it was the greatest act of faith was because He had the most to lose. The writer of Hebrews says, "If you need a model of faith, look at Jesus. He went through an incredible crisis, but in believing God He was victorious."

B. Our Focus

The phrase "looking unto Jesus" in the Greek literally reads "to look away to Jesus." Where a person has his focus is important. For example, when my dad was teaching me how to hit a baseball, he'd say, "You can't hit the baseball unless you keep your eye on the ball." When we played basketball he'd say, "You can't make a basket unless you keep your eye on the basket."

The same is true in the Christian life. Your focal point must be beyond yourself. In fact, the sooner you get your eyes off yourself the better off you are. I disagree with the constant discussion about Christian self-analysis and introspection—where we are always analyzing our spiritual problems. We get so wrapped up in watching ourselves that it's like trying to drive a car while we're watching the pedals. The sooner you get your eyes off yourself and focused on Jesus Christ the better off you'll be.

When you run a race, you don't look at your feet. So it is that we are to look to Jesus. Why? Because He is the perfect pattern, the perfect model, the perfect example. You're not even to look at the other runners—just at Christ.

Verse 2 says that Christ is the "author and finisher of our faith." The word translated "author" is the Greek word *arche-*

gos and means "originator, pioneer, leader, primogenitor, supreme." In other words, Christ is the chief leader of faith, greater than any example in Hebrews 11—or anywhere else. The word *finisher* is the Greek word *teleion* and means "to carry through to completion, to make perfect or complete." He is the chief example of one who carried faith to its completion. He lived by perfect faith from beginning to end.

V. THE END (v. 2*b*)

"Who for the joy that was set before Him endured the cross, despising the shame, and is set down at the right hand of the throne of God."

What's at the end of the race? What do we get if we win? Two things—joy and triumph. Joy is subjective; triumph is objective. Joy is that great exhilarating feeling that you have won, and triumph is the actual reward of God. An athlete knows that there is nothing equal to the thrill of winning. It isn't the medal or the trophy—or anything else—it's just the winning, the exhilaration of victory. So there is the joy of victory as well as the reward of God. In the case of Christ, His reward was that He was seated at the right hand of the Father. And in the case of the Christian, there are five crowns that can be ours: an incorruptible crown (1 Cor. 9:25), a crown of rejoicing (1 Thess. 2:19), a crown of righteousness (2 Tim. 4:8), a crown of life (James 1:12), and a crown of glory (1 Pet. 5:4).

Joy and triumph aren't necessarily just in the future. Ultimately, the real joy and the reward is in heaven with Christ, but here and now we can experience a great sense of joy and a tremendous sense of triumph when we win the victory over temptation. We get a little taste of what the ultimate joy and the ultimate victory is going to be.

VI. THE EXHORTATION (vv. 3-4)

Having presented this powerful appeal to get into the race and run it, the writer of Hebrews knows there are going to be some people who are going to say, "Well, you know, it's not easy being a Christian. I'm abused at the water cooler. . . . They short me on paper clips. . . . My philosophy teacher attacks my beliefs in class. . . . My husband makes our home difficult. . . . It's getting harder and harder to be a Christian in our society because we're getting close to the end times," and so on. Verses 3-4 say, "For consider him that endured such contradiction of sinners against himself, lest ye be wearied and faint in your minds. Ye have not yet resisted unto blood, striving against sin." In other words he is saying, "I don't see any of you bleeding. It may be a little rough at the water cooler, and you may get hassled in your philosophy class, but you haven't been crucified yet like Someone I know."

Do you see where his exhortation comes from? When you start thinking it's too tough to live the Christian life, consider One who endured such a contradiction of sinners against Himself that He went as far as death—and realize you haven't gone that far yet. Just realize that you don't have it so difficult. You haven't been burned at the stake, beheaded, or thrown to a lion. You're not hiding in mountains, dens, and caves. You haven't been sawed in half or had your eyes gouged out. When you start getting weary and faint, consider Jesus Christ who endured such contradiction of sinners. And if His life of faith had triumph and victory, they can be yours too.

If you're not in the race, get in it! There's a prize out there for you—joy and triumph. And, Christian, since you're in the race, run it with all you've got!

Focusing on the Facts

1. What are some of the figures of speech used in the New Testament to describe the Christian life (see p. 156)?
2. True or false: When the writer of Hebrews uses the word *us*, he is addressing fellow believers exclusively (see p. 157).
3. Describe the three categories of readers addressed in the book of Hebrews (see pp. 157-58).
4. Is it easy to live the Christian life? Explain (see p. 160).
5. What does it take to excel in the life of faith (see pp. 160-61)?
6. Who are the "cloud of witnesses" (Heb. 12:1; see pp. 161-62)?
7. What was the single greatest factor that hindered Jewish people from coming to Christ (see p. 163)?
8. What sin has the most devastating effect on faith (see p. 164)?
9. True or false: Every sin we commit can be traced ultimately to unbelief (see p. 164).

10. Why was Jesus' becoming man and dying for our sins the greatest act of faith ever (see pp. 164-65)?
11. What should we focus on as we run the Christian race (see p. 165)?
12. What are the prizes for those who successfully run the Christian race (see p. 166)?
13. What should we do when we believe the Christian race is getting too difficult (see p. 167)?

Pondering the Principles

1. One group that the writer of Hebrews addressed were fence-sitters—those who believed the gospel but had not acted on it. Can you think of some people you know who are sitting on the fence? Ask God to give you insight into what is keeping them from Christ. Perhaps they face ostracism from their families and friends or are unwilling to give up some sin they're involved with. Whatever it is, ask God to give you boldness to confront them with the truth that "now is the day of salvation" (2 Cor. 6:2).

2. When we feel weak and discouraged, it is often helpful to look at the lives of great men of God. We've been doing that all through our study of Hebrews 11. We have seen that they faced the same kinds of struggles and temptations we do and have learned how they overcame them. When was the last time you read the biography of one of the great men or women in church history? If you can't remember, why not pay your local Christian bookstore or church library a visit and get a biography of someone whose life is worthy of emulation. You'll be glad you did!

Scripture Index

Topical Index

ordinary nature of, 93-95

Jacob
  deceit of, 98-99
  faith of, 99-101
Jephthah, faith of, 147
Jeremiah, faith of, 149
Joseph, faith of, 101-2, 149
Joshua, faith of, 140-43
Joy. See Happiness
Judgment, mercy inherent in,
    66-67. See also God, jus-
    tice of questioned

Kerkut, G. A., 19
Kierkegaard, Søren, 16

Legalism, 163
Longevity, possible explanation
    of early human, 61

Materialism. See World, riches
    of
Maturity, a measure of Chris-
    tian, 79, 107
Meaning in life. See Faith
Methuselah, significance of
    name, 67
Moffatt, James, 24
Money. See World, riches of
Moses
  beauty of, 131
  faith of, 9-10, 106-16, 121-34
  training of, 111
Music, 17

Narrowmindedness, rebuking
    accusations of, 30
Nationality, unimportance of,
    42
Noah
  days of, 68-69
  faith of, 12-13, 57-69

message of, 64-69
  See also Ark, the

Obedience. See Faith, life of
Origins. See Evolution,
    Philosophy

Patience. See Faith, patience of
Persecution. See World, perse-
    cution of
Philosophy, 16-17, 18-19, 21
Pride, humbling of, 142
Promises of God. See God,
    promises of
Provision of God. See God, pro-
    vision of
Psychology, danger of intro-
    spection, 165

Rahab, faith of, 143-45
Rapture, the. See Enoch, trans-
    lation of
Rationalism, 16-17, 20
Rationality, 45
Reconciliation, 48-49
Reincarnation, appeal of, 17
Religion
  beginning of false, 28-29
  God's feelings about, 42
  See also Legalism, Works
Repentance, remorse vs., 34
Revelation, 20
Russell, Bertrand, 18-19

Sacrifices
  initiation of, 29-31, 41
  provision of. See God, provi-
    sion of
  See also Worship
Salvation, only way to, 47-48.
    See also Faith, saving;
    Reconciliation
Samson, faith of, 146-47